PUNCHING UP

PUBLISH A BOOK THAT MARTIAL ARTISTS WILL WANT TO OWN

(and actually read)

Copyright © 2024 by Kris Wilder and Lawrence A. Kane.

Cover design and interior layout by Kami Miller.

Illustrations by Kris Wilder.

All rights reserved. No part of this publication may be reproduced, distributed or transmitted in any form or by any means, including photocopying, recording, or other electronic or mechanical methods, without the prior written permission of the publisher, except in the case of brief quotations embodied in critical reviews and certain other noncommercial uses permitted by copyright law. For permission requests, contact the authors via email: Kris Wilder (kriswilder@kriswilder.com) or Lawrence Kane (lakane@ix.netcom.com).

Stickman Publications, Inc. Seattle, WA 98126

ISBN-13: 979-8-9855617-8-4

Disclaimer: Information in this book is distributed "As Is," without warranty. Nothing in this document constitutes a legal opinion nor should any of its contents be treated as such. Neither the authors nor the publisher shall have any liability with respect to information contained herein. Further, neither the authors nor the publisher have any control over or assume any responsibility for websites or external resources referenced in this book.

PUNCHING UP

PUBLISH A BOOK THAT MARTIAL ARTISTS WILL WANT TO OWN

(and actually read)

Kris Wilder & Lawrence A. Kane

Explore more books from the authors:

Kris Wilder and Lawrence Kane are the bestselling, award-winning authors of *Musashi's Dokkodo*, *The Little Black Book of Violence*, *10 Rules of Karate, Dude*, *The World's Gonna Punch You in the Face*, and *Martial Arts and Your Life*, among numerous other titles. Discover more below...

Kris Wilder

Lawrence A. Kane

Table of Contents

Introduction	ix
Your Sisyphean Challenge	1
Green as Pool Table	7
Know Your Motivation	15
Find Your Voice	25
Know Your Audience	35
Word Count	43
Preparation	49
Create Compelling Value	55
Look at Me, I Wrote a Book!	67
Abandon The "Make-a-Fist Book"	77
Setting a Writing Schedule	83
"Writer's Block" is for Losers	91
Jeweler's Loop Reviews	95
Trusted and Untruthful Feeback	101
Cover Art	107
Audio Books	115
You Need a Website — Not!	123
How You Publish Matters	127
Protect Your Copyright	139
Insider Info	145
Paying it Forward	155
Conclusion	163
About the Authors	169

Introduction

"A person who publishes a book willfully appears before the populace with his pants down. If it is a good book nothing can hurt him. If it is a bad book nothing can help him."

— Edna St. Vincent Millay

So, you wanna write a book…

The diocesan convention Kris attended was held at a hotel, with conference rooms packed full of religious people gathered to conduct church business while strengthening their fellowship. Breakout groups, presentations, mission statements, and other administrivia all formed a cocktail of discomfort for him. Seeking some relief from the bureaucracy, Kris wandered into the vendor section of the gathering.

The sellers were many, and largely what he had expected, purveyors of crosses, candles, coffee, and croissants. Rounding the final corner of the vendor's row, Kris spotted a retired priest sitting behind a stack of books. Making eye contact, the priest smiled Kris's way and Kris returned the gesture, adding a small wave. He felt compelled to wander over to the guy's table for politeness's sake if nothing else. He wasn't looking to buy a book.

That priest had all the markers of a first-time author. He not only sat next to a veritable mountain of books, but also had boxes packed with additional copies under the table. Kris had seen much the same thing at martial arts seminars over the years, the stack of books for sale, the nervous tension, the polite eye contact... and the complete lack of customers interested in buying anything. While there were dozens of shoppers wandering through the vendor marketplace, few even glanced at the priest's table.

"How are you?"

Kris quickly confirmed that the affable and engaging priest was a first-time author. It checked out and the conversation went from bad to... well, you know. You see that priest had written a fictionalized account of Jesus's life. Not heretical or theological, the book delved deeply into the culture, customs, and traditions in the Middle East at the time when Jesus grew up. The author had gone so far as to methodically describe the type of tile used in the entryways of high-end homes two thousand years ago.

While he'd done his research, that book was a niche work if ever there was one. It was a religious volume written by a first-time author for sale at a Christian convention. That's aimed at a small subsection of the marketplace.

Perhaps if that priest had a "marquee" name that folks more broadly would have recognized, say a former pope, he would have attracted a larger potential audience, but even at the diocesan convention, few folks had heard of him. Is it possible to get any smaller exposure? That's akin to a book penned by Chuck Norris versus one written by *Sensei* Harry Schweenwacke, you already know who's more likely to have a bestseller irrespective of who's a better author.

This was an earnest old man who had put his heart and soul into his work and had a garage full of unsold books for his efforts, volumes he was eventually going to have to give away to whoever would take one to have a place to park his car. Sadly, he had bought into the publisher's pitch. "You know if you print a thousand copies you get a discount, and that means more money for you in the long run."

That priest had started behind the proverbial eight ball. In becoming a writer, he listened to people who didn't have his best interests at heart. "Hey besides the books you need business cards, mugs, bookmarks, t-shirts… and a web site! We'll pull it all together for you for you, for the low, low price of just…" In the vernacular of the con man, they saw that priest coming.

After a short conversation Kris bought one of the priest's books out of pity. He skimmed through it once, never actually reading it. It may have wound up at Goodwill, or perhaps it's buried somewhere in the basement, but whatever happened to the book Kris doesn't miss it. He does, however, still feel sorry for that guy.

Like that priest, you want to become a writer. You think you know how. You're not dumb, you can figure this out, right? "I'll do my research," you say. Sure, you can, just like we did. Know, however, that many of the research sources are tainted, obfuscated, and chocked full of deception.

Back in the day when we first started writing simply being published meant around 3,500 sales as that's what it took to stock the brick-and-mortar booksellers across the country. Nowadays most of those establishments have gone out of business. The rise of print-on-demand was a sea change for the publishing industry. Amazon alone is responsible for over half the worldwide sales from the Big Five publishers[1] and controls roughly 70% to 80% of all book distribution in the United States. And, unlike a couple decades ago, the average book written today is forecast to sell less than 250 copies over its lifetime.

If we told you how much money we've left on the table or flat-out lost because of our choices it would curl your toes. Further, it would embarrass us... Suffice it to say that we've learned a lot along the way and those painful lessons can foment your success.

Certainly, we will make you far, far more productive than that pathetic priest at the end of the hallway who got a pity sale from Kris at the diocesan convention. We are going to save you from becoming the equivalent of a person standing at a freeway entrance with a cardboard sign selling your book for 98.5% off.

Here's the topline. To be a successful author, you must:

- Know your audience
- Create something of value (e.g., inspire, educate, entertain)
- Produce an exceptional title that garners attention
- Create a cover that will stand out from the crowd
- Thoughtfully consider which channel(s) to leverage to get your work into the marketplace
- Make an informed decision on how to publish (e.g., traditional vs. niche vs. self-pub)
- Protect your copyright
- Always, always, always market your work

We've done all that and more. And we'll teach you how. Read on...

---

1 Book publishing is dominated by a handful of companies known as the Big Five, including Hachette Book Group, HarperCollins, Macmillan Publishers, Penguin Random House, and Simon & Schuster, who collectively control roughly 80% of the US trade book market.

Your Sisyphean Challenge

"None of us would choose to be Sisyphus; yet in a sense, we all are."
— Joko Beck

It's not easy, get ready.

Books by the Numbers

According to a recent survey, 81% of Americans believe they have a book in them. Since you picked this up, you're obviously one of them. We're going to be straight with you, getting published is easy. In fact, over 2,300,000 new titles are released through self-publishing, niche, independent, and non-traditional publishers on an annual basis. The challenge is that most of them are crap. An additional 300,000 new titles or thereabouts are released through the Big Five traditional publishing houses every year too. They're not only better quality in general, but they also tend to be far better marketed as well. So yeah, getting published is easy, but putting out something that folks hear about and want to own is hard.

In this book we'll share insider secrets to help you succeed.

It's not just the market that's tough, it takes discipline to get your work into the marketplace. While 81% of Americans believe they have a book in them, a mere 15% have started writing. And only 6% have gotten halfway through. In fact, roughly 1.8% of aspiring writers get published.[2] And, while it's nice to have your work out in the world, and a book can add gravitas to other endeavors, less than 6% of published authors earn a living from their writing.[3]

Despite all that, if you're really driven to get your book published, we'll show you how to make that happen. Before we do, let's geek out on challenges inherent in the in the process:

- ⇨ Adjusting for inflation, book industry revenues declined 38% between 2000 and 2022 and are projected to continue that downward trend over the next decade
- ⇨ Based on ISBN registrations[4], 3,931,270 books were published in 2022, yet new titles accounted for only 32% of retail book sales
- ⇨ Despite the growth of audio and e-books, physical books accounted for 76.42% of industry revenue in 2022 and are expected to dominate all other mediums in sales for the next decade
- ⇨ Less than 5% of all books ever published have sold more than 5,000 copies
- ⇨ The average book written today is forecast to sell less than 250 copies over its lifetime
- ⇨ Most book marketing today is done by authors not publishers regardless of how the work is published

Now for some good news. While some of the most famous authors are novelists like Tom Clancy, C. S. Lewis, Agatha Christie, Danielle Steel, Stephen King, Harold Robbins,

---

2   Much lower if we don't count self-publishing.

3   Only 1.3% of traditionally published authors, 0.7% of self-published authors, and 5.7% of hybrid authors earn over $100,000 a year from their work.

4   ISBN stands for International Standard Book Number, an identifier assigned to all books and book-like publications that are published internationally. ISBNs do not directly equate to unique titles as, for example, hardcovers and softcover versions of the same book have different ISBNs.

and J. K. Rowling, nonfiction writing is counterintuitively more profitable. In part this is because non-fiction is prone to generating multiple revenue streams such as through books, online courses, merchandise sales, etc. This dynamic creates an opportunity for martial artists that other writers are less able to take advantage of. Sure, most of us don't do this for the money alone, but our time is valuable and creating something that folks want to own and refer back to over and over again is both rewarding and inherently valuable.

It's Difficult, but not Futile

In Greek mythology Sisyphus was the King of Ephyra, later known as Corinth. "The craftiest of men," according to Homer, he was a murderous tyrant whose violation of sacred traditions angered the gods Zues and Hades. After escaping death twice he was condemned to eternal punishment in Tartarus, the lowest region of the underworld, where he would forever be forced to roll a massive boulder up a steep hill. Whenever he neared the top, the weight of the rock would overwhelm him and the boulder would come crashing back to the bottom, forcing him to start over. Sisyphean challenges, therefore, are both difficult and futile.

Your writing journey will feel like a Sisyphean challenge. It's not, not really, but it will feel that way. You'll make progress on a passage or chapter one day only to find yourself staring at that proverbial boulder at the bottom of the steep hill the next morning. You will feel little if any sense of accomplishment, but never fear, you're not an evil tyrant like Sisyphus. You haven't been condemned to hell. If you embrace the grind you are going to make it over the crest of the hill one day.

Just as a black belt is a white belt who never gave up, if you keep plugging away and you will without a doubt complete your task. You will publish a book that martial artists will want to own, read, and refer to. We'll show you how to do that as effectively and efficiently as possible.

Green as Pool Table

"I'm just green as a pool table, you know I'm twice as square."

— George "Buddy" Guy

**You think you know,
but you don't.**

Learn From our Mistakes and Successes

There are numerous sources of advice on how to get published you could choose from, so why listen to us? We have proof in the market, not some quick e-book sold on Instagram designed to inflate your ego while separating you from your hard-earned money. Further we were once just like the great blues guitarist Buddy Guy, as "green as a pool table," and by reading this volume you can learn from our mistakes so that you won't have to figure out the hard way how to get ahead in the book business.

Over the last two decades we've published over 30 acclaimed works in half a dozen languages, most of which are bestsellers.[5] We started with a specialty martial arts publisher and then worked with one of the Big Five traditional publishers before creating our own publishing house, Stickman Publications, so we know the industry and can intelligently speak to the pros and cons of traditional

---

5   Don't get too excited, that just means we sold more than 5,000 copies of each one of them.

publishers, independent publishers, self-publishing aggregators, self-publishing retail channels, hybrid publishing, self-publishing, and author services providers.

We have a long track record. Even though we primarily write for a niche market, let's face it martial arts are not exactly mainstream, *The Little Black Book of Violence* made it to #13 on all of Amazon way back in 2010 and more recently *Musashi's Dokkodo* was the #1 bestselling book in Martial Arts on Amazon for 36 weeks in a row.

As you can see from the chart on the left, which is indicative of virtually any title not just the one shown, book sales tend to fall off over time. Each new title you release can cause a spike in your back catalog, assuming you're staying in the same genre or an adjacency that attracts largely the same fan base, but even with these bumps the overall trend is declining.

This downward curve isn't just something that happens to us, it has been accelerating for virtually all authors over time due to dynamics of the modern marketplace. That's why traditional publishers focus more marketing and advertising dollars on new releases than they do on established titles.

Books are, and were, a Luxury

At one time in history books were rare, valuable, handwritten works that few could afford let alone read. The manuscripts were hand-copied on vellum, a parchment made of calfskin. We can all conjure the image of monks hunkered over their wooden desks, quill in hand, meticulously copying each document by candlelight... which is exactly what happened for centuries.

Handmade paper, quill, and ink writing were the means and the method by which valuable knowledge was replicated and distributed. Then Johannes Gensfleisch zur Laden zum Gutenberg (1393 - 1468) changed the world with his movable-type printing press and the mass production of books it enabled. Gutenberg had no idea, way back in 1439 (give or take a year), that roughly three million books a year would be produced nowadays because of his invention, the ancient ancestor of print-on-demand publishing.

Books used to be a luxury item. Access was a challenge and being able to read them was another challenge. The math was simple, if you were both rich and educated your library could become a sign of your status.

You'd think the world has changed substantially in the last 585+ years, but when it comes to books in many ways it has not. You see, today books are generally not expensive. Outside the rare book market, academic journals, medical periodicals, and law books, they are a dime a baker's dozen. It's not the cost that's the primary factor today, yet books are becoming rare once again for a variety of different reasons.

Short Attention Span Theater

One reason books are becoming rare again is that for the most part recreational reading is falling out of favor with younger people. Humans are visual animals, so when we can acquire the information we want on video, using YouTube, or social media, why read old school? This helps explain why industry revenues have dropped 38% over the last couple of decades,[6] despite a cumulative price increase of 69.95% due to inflation during that time.

Second, often for consumers it's all about the information, not the experience. "Give me what I need quickly so I can make a decision, a choice, or move forward now." This quick-shot information is fine in many instances, but loss of context is common. This is pure predator behavior, obtaining

---

6   This data is from 2000 to 2022.

the resource with the least expenditure of time and energy. You already knew that as a martial artist.

This dynamic shouldn't keep you from writing, but it should encourage you to do so wisely. For example, longer books have less bang for the proverbial buck. It's not only that they take longer to get into the marketplace, but also that many folks simply won't embrace them. And larger books generate reduced royalties per page than smaller ones due to publishing costs, even an e-book or audiobook format.

You're making the first smart move already by reading this book and learning from our mistakes. Sadly, our miscalculations were many, we largely blazed our trail rather than following in others' footsteps, but we learned from our errors, so you won't have to repeat our mistakes. You can make your own.

Options

Despite being in a fluid market, with rules, risks, and opportunities changing often, we're confident in our ability to steer you in the right direction. Nevertheless, we know that you're going to ignore some of what we tell you. That's okay, you are an adult. Glean what you want, use what you wish to use, and discard the rest.

What makes this book different than an online course? We're not trying to sell you anything other than this resource you already bought or borrowed from someone else, but rather lay out your options and let you choose the best direction to proceed based on your individual needs. We are going to share real-world stories to underscore why certain ideas are great moves in the publishing world. And we will also share a few flat-out horror stories too.

You are serious, we respect that. You want a book, and we'll teach you how to write one and get it published. While our focus is on martial arts books, our advice applies to publishing nearly any genre. We've written about leadership, procurement, and self-help too. Welcome to the unvarnished, brutal, and rewarding world of writing a book.

Now, let's get to work...

Know Your Motivation

"This show is for me, and people like me, that like the things I like."

— Dana Gould

Write for us. You know, you and me.

Three Reasons

Here are three common reasons why people choose to write a book:

- ⇨ You get to call yourself an author
- ⇨ You want to make money
- ⇨ You have information that you believe needs preserving for others

You can think of those three motives as a Venn diagram, one reason is not excluded from the others. They can touch and overlap. If you are of the first category, you get to call yourself an author. If your desire to have your name on the front of a book is important, go right ahead. Know that a million people are doing the same, literally 3 to 4 million per year and growing. Just because you write it does not by any means indicate that anyone will want to buy your work.

As we mentioned previously, the average book published today sells less than 250 copies over its lifetime, meaning that most books are really nothing more than vanity projects. A vanity project is writing a book primarily based on the motivation of being able to say you're an author, having your name on the cover.

Rude but True

At a holiday party last year Kris was introduced by a friend to a new acquaintance. In the meeting the host pointed to the fact that Kris had written a book. The reply from the new acquaintance was stunning in its directness, and true. She said, "Anybody can be an author now." Rude, sure, but 100% right.

In Kris's defense, the host interjected, "He has a publisher, one of the big ones." The defense by the host was gracious, implying that Kris's book created value, wasn't some self-published garbage, but the message was blunt and still stood. He could see the unvoiced response on the acquaintance's face, "Whatever."

If your motivation is to be able to say, "I'm an Author," great. Don't expect anybody to care because they won't. Well, maybe your mom will... But there is an alternate vision. We aim for more than that, and you should too.

Books as Business Card Ventures

While vanity projects are nice, business card ventures are better. That ties a strategic incentive to the work. In other words, writing a book to have your name on the cover because you want it to be part of your business suite, that's a great move. For example, while Lawrence primarily writes about martial arts, self-defense, violence in society, and related subjects, he's also written and contributed to books on procurement, contracting, leadership, and various other business subjects, then used them as resume-fodder to land a better job. In many fields—academia, business, and law, to name a few—being a published author creates a real advantage.

If you intend to use your book as a business card, know this and act accordingly in your project's development. When you get done with your book, you will have a big business card, one that people will be hesitant to throw away. Think of it as branding. Your book(s) becomes part of your business, your public identity. Done right it adds gravitas in much the same way an industry award or advanced degree often will.

In the martial arts world, you can turn your book into a brand extension, making it available to your classes, seminars, or as an addition to your other offerings. An example of this use could be to give the book away after an event or sell it at a deep discount to attendees. This formula adds value to the experience, hence is used by business executives and course promoters from self-help to needlepoint. It is a good tactic in part because it helps attendees both remember what they learned and subtly incentivizes them to tell their friends about it. That's far better than doing a vanity project to get your name on the cover of a book.

If you want to make money, well so does the publisher, and they get the first bite at the apple. You get less. The amounts vary from company to company, but a publisher is rolling the dice. If they're willing to sign a deal, they are making a bet on you, and because of the calculated risk they are going to take a hefty cut to safeguard their investment. Further, you can take it or leave it. They are a business.

We'll get into this in more detail later, but if you go through a traditional publisher, they own the royalties and pay you based on a portion of sales. If you self-publish, on the other hand, you own the royalties, sans channel residuals, and for all intents and purposes pay yourself.

Consequently, if you self-publish, say on Amazon, Scribd, Smashwords, or Books-A-Million, you will get more return on each sale, but you won't get the kind of boost a traditional publisher or niche publishing house will give you in terms of market penetration. And, you won't get the help, you'll need to do the editing, layout, marketing, advertising, and all the rest yourself.

No matter what you do, don't expect to get rich. Even though we've sold hundreds of thousands of books, if you add up all the time we've spent on writing, editing, marketing, and the like, we made way less than minimum wage on royalties from our work, which brings us to the next motivation, preservation of knowledge.

Preserving Valuable Information

Another form of a book in the publishing world is preserving information for the future, an honorable goal. There is a reason that libraries need support from tax dollars, they cannot stand on their own. The same formula exists for museums. So, if you're writing a museum piece you must understand that most people won't want to pay for what you have written. Sure, people visit museums on occasion, but make no mistake, no museum on earth doesn't need some form of subsidy. You as the author will get no such subvention.

If you go into this version of a book with your eyes wide open, you will be fine. Your expectations will be realistic. Know too, that there is a subspecies of "information preservation" books, and they're called manuals. Manuals will not sell outside of your narrow and specific target market, which is almost always a niche of a niche. In many instances they're better given away than sold, since the broader the distribution the better preservation of the information they impart.

Mission Creep

What happens with these preservation-type books is that without due diligence they experience mission creep. These books tend to start as a manual, and the initial material is good. The next leap is the idea that "This should be for everybody if only they knew!" Do yourself a favor and switch to decaf.

Refocus yourself. Keep the initial goal firmly in mind or you will waste time and money, perhaps never even completing your work. A manual with mission creep often contains extraneous photos and illustrations, most of which do nothing to increase their value. In the martial arts genre, they tend to meander off into lineage, checklists, positions, and other unnecessary filler. Then there is an emphasis on your organization and style, which might be compelling to a potential audience if your name is Chuck Norris, but almost certainly not if it's *Sensei* Harry Schweenwacke. Run away from the mission creep. If you are writing a manual, write a manual.

For Kris's *dojo*, he has a manual. That manual is available on his website for any student to download in PDF format. In fact, anybody with the link can access it, it is not locked away behind a firewall. Despite being told about it, only a handful of students have ever accessed that manual.

It doesn't matter that Kris is a Martial Arts Hall of Fame member who's published 32 books. It doesn't matter that he has been interviewed by CNN, FOX, The Huffington Post, Thrillist, Nickelodeon, and Howard Stern either. Few folks want a copy of his *dojo* manual. Sure, Kris is famous, but people prefer one-to-one education and information. This is the first choice of most folks, and it is a good thing. Be aware of this. A manual is generally received as well as cold eggs at breakfast.

The bottom line is that manuals don't sell, but they are valuable. That's why Kris gives his away.

Dry but Useful... to Those Who Care

As a martial artist you know that martial arts are powerful and transformative. We all agree. Here are the cold hard facts, however, nobody cares about what your studies have done for you. Well, to be fair some people—your friends, and your family—may care, but paying customers don't care. Think of it as writing a book on what it took to earn your Ph.D. People would rather hear about your last haircut.

Most people walk past the benefit we have earned from our studies. They walk past without a nod in the general direction of the undeniable improvement in our lives. Why would a random stranger take an interest in your life? The people closest to you have difficulty in seeing the benefits of martial arts unless they're fellow martial artists and possibly not even then.

This is because martial arts have become so ingrained in your existence that they have become a backdrop. It is like whitetail deer season in Texas[7]. To the family of a deer hunter, the season opens and it closes. During that time, they know the hunter is out hunting, and they carry on with their lives. It is the default.

The martial arts information you have assembled is valuable to you because it is transformative. Not so much for others. Think of it this way: people who take interest in philosophy are philosophy students. Or engaged in autodidacticism. Both are small markets. If you're looking to pass on some hard-earned wisdom to make your students' lives better, good. If you are using the writing process to coalesce and solidify what you've learned, also good. Go write that manuscript, but realize that it's a manual not a book.

Be aware of the context and know that the content will work against your book's chances of success. The likelihood of your book becoming the next *How to Win Friends and Influence People* is remote. Like that priest we described in the introduction, you're squarely in a triple niche market, if not worse. The most noteworthy things about that priest's book are the facts that Kris can't remember the title and never actually read it. He seemed like a good dude though...

Think about which of the above categories your proposed book falls into. Do you want to be able to call yourself an author, make money, preserve vital knowledge, or some combination of the three? Whatever reason(s) you have chosen, know that to get a good book, one that will resonate with your audience, is going to be brutal. That means a mountain of work from you.

Journey to The Moon

Kris attended an event with Dan Millman, author of *Way of the Peaceful Warrior*. Millman described the book writing

---

7   The Texas Parks & Wildlife Department estimates that there are around 900,000 hunters in the state, which means that a lot of folks disappear into the woods between early November and late January.

process like an astronaut going to the moon. The initial launch is exciting, but that soon gives way to the long drudgery of the flight. Excitement resumes upon approach to the moon, then wanes again when circling around the dark side where you are alone. That drudgery is repeated along the return trip, followed by a resurgence of enthusiasm at re-entry with the final touchdown.

That analogy is accurate.

Now with that little ray of sunshine, let's move on to cover the mechanics of getting your book out into the world.

Find Your Voice

"Being different is good; embrace it."

— Simon Cowell

Why embrace an imitation when you can have the real thing?

You can break martial arts books down into subcategories such as reference manuals, philosophical treatises, self-help books, style specific instructional workbooks, or historical works, to name just a few. In fact, virtually all aspects of human existence can be written through the prism of martial arts, so your opportunities are legion. In order to get started it is helpful to break this down into two big categories that affect how you proceed: Are you going to be clinical or are you going to be conversational?

In making this choice you need to establish what you believe to be your voice. Here's an example of what we experienced as a business team, it is unique to us, but we share it to get you thinking about yourself...

One plus One Equals Three

Lawrence grew up in a suburban environment next to a large city, while Kris grew up on a farm. Lawrence has one sister and Kris has one brother. Lawrence went to a university, while Kris went to a state college. Lawrence is Jewish. Kris is Christian. Lawrence's father was an aerospace engineer, whereas Kris's father was a farmer. The list goes on about the differences, they're numerous, and they create a diversity of experience, thought process, and opinion that we leverage to make our works stronger. It's the old 1 + 1 = 3 thing. Together we're better than either one of us is individually. That's why so many of our books are co-written.

These differences are valuable assets in shaping the vision for our books. We lean into each other's strengths and weaknesses. Lawrence is direct, thorough, and precise. Kris is more experiential, with a raging case of dyslexia. We balance each other, we build on one another. For example, often it's Kris who comes up with the idea for a new project and Lawrence who refines it. Kris does the art, and Lawrence does the science.

Create a Writing Persona

This blend brings us a voice. When you read our books, you're not experiencing Lawrence or Kris, but rather a combination of the two that is intentional. If you've read multiple books we've written, you have undoubtedly discovered that this "voice" varies from work to work. We create a persona taken from our collective experience who's best able to communicate the subject matter to its intended audience.

Dude, The World's Gonna Punch You in the Face was "written" by that wise uncle you love to hang out with. He can tell it to you straight in ways that others can't or won't. As an at-risk youth he understands your world, he'll connect without patronizing or condescending.

Contrast that with *Sensei Mentor Teacher Coach* which was "penned" by a certified life coach and international business executive who has counseled college graduates entering the

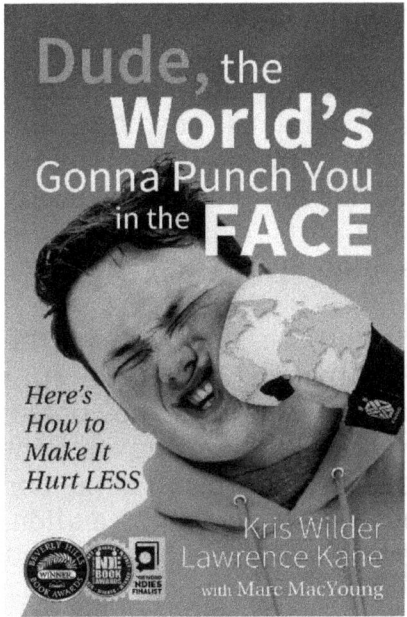 

workforce, guided early career professionals through job progressions, helped military personnel transition to the corporate world, and taught nonprofit organizations how to improve the efficacy of their philanthropic efforts. It's a book about mentoring by guys who have been there, done that, and can teach you how.

As you can see, these are two divergent books aimed at different audiences, each using a voice appropriate for the readership. Whether writing solo or in partnership, do the same thing. Create a writing persona, crafting a voice that will resonate with the folks who need what you have to say.

Leverage Your Authentic Voice

It's essential to understand your unadulterated voice. The movies of Wes Anderson (e.g., *Rushmore, Moonrise Kingdom*) are symmetrical. Anderson's films are made-up of primary colors and hyper-balanced scenes. The work of David Lynch (e.g., *Blue Velvet, Mulholland Drive*), on the other hand, are disturbing in their imagery. Lynch's films lack overt clarity in motivation and dive into symbology. No one would ever confuse Anderson for Lynch. Their voices are unique, different.

You are a product of your environment, like we are. Use it, it is a strength. You have opinions, positions, and preferences. Do not shy away from them. If you decide to write for everybody you write for no one. Your voice is your perspective, a calling card of sorts. If it's unique and interesting, it drives sales. If it's milquetoast, well you know how that ends...

Be you, but be the best you to tell the story, impart the information your audience is looking for. And make sure everything you say and do publicly reinforces that image you wish your readers to perceive. Despite tailoring our joint writing voice to the needs of each work, we're still being our authentic selves. There's no smokescreen, no disinformation.

We do us. You do you. Make it real, make it appealing, and make it thought-provoking.

The Hazards of AI

That leads us to a warning about technology, it is a tool, not a crutch... Using it carries a variety of risks, including muddling your voice. You can do you better than any computer can do you. Additionally, using the right technology in the wrong way carries the very real risk of copyright infringement, which will bring you serious trouble.

In the early days of ChatGPT someone posted an ad on LinkedIn about a book they'd "written" with Artificial Intelligence (AI). Included in their advertisement was an excerpt from the book, which included a quotation that we had published, and copyrighted, in 2009.

Clearly the machine had learned from internet postings, many of which referred to our bestselling book, but since there are no Intellectual Property (IP) safeguards in the system neither the AI nor the "author" knew that, nor cared apparently. That's problematic.

Lawrence DM'd the author, informing him that it was okay to use the quote from our book but also informing him that he needed to cite the source. This is standard etiquette in the industry and helps authors assure compliance with Section 107 of the Copyright Act, which specifies four factors of fair use legal doctrine. Rather than complying, which would have been simple and easy to do, that guy blocked him, so Lawrence turned to Amazon, through whom the plagiarist had published, for remediation.

Long story short, that book was removed from the site and demonetized. Additionally, Amazon added an AI validation check along with their standard copyright verification in KDP, their publishing tool, caused no doubt by numerous situations where stolen IP was brought to their attention.

How to Do it Right

To be clear, using AI to write a book is not the same as writing a book. ChatGPT or any other form of AI goes out across the world-wide-web scraping information. Then it coalesces what it finds into a cogent summary. This sounds simple, it sounds easy, but in leveraging the machine you're not writing a book. You are not creating. You are not sharing your unique vision. All you're doing is sourcing public information, and that is a regression to the mean. This technique makes you average; at best you have become a file clerk, not a real author.

There are emerging AI companies like perplexity.ai who both cite sources and walk you through a series of questions to help ferret out legitimate answers to your queries. Nevertheless, if you're going to leverage AI to do your research, independently fact check what you've found. AI is only as good as the data that the machine "learns" from, and let's face it, much of the world wide web is a steaming pool of rubbish.

Keep in mind that AI tends to "hallucinate," creating fake images or conjuring phony information. These errors are caused by a variety of factors, including insufficient training data, circular references, incorrect assumptions in the model, and biases in the data used to train the model. If you publish that garbage, at best it will materially harm your reputation.

In 2023 a New York federal judge sanctioned attorneys who used ChatGPT to create legal briefs that included fake citations, quotes, and non-existent court opinions. Judge P. Kevin Castel told CNBC that the attorneys, Peter LoDuca and Steven Schwartz, "Abandoned their responsibilities and then continued to stand by the fake opinions after judicial orders called their existence into question." He ordered both attorneys, along with their law firm Levidow, Levidow & Oberman, to pay $5,000 in fines apiece. Ethical breaches like that are a good way for lawyers to get suspended or debarred.

Dangers of AI aside, the reason we all have *Tao of Jeet Kune Do* on our bookshelves is because Bruce Lee wrote it. We want to know what Bruce Lee had to say. By the time ChatGPT or any other AI can do that we'll all either be dodging terminators and praying for John Connor or sipping margaritas on a beach somewhere without a care in the world. While data scientists, technologists, and ethicists figure that future out, suffice it to say that without your unique, human voice your book won't be worth the paper it's printed on or the electrons it's displayed with. There are many legitimate uses for AI but ghostwriting a book is not one of them.

The Big Flow and Small Card

Here's an action we suggest you undertake to better understand your voice. Write down who you are as a martial artist. Avoid bullet points and editing. Go with the flow. Use as many or as few words as you need. We call this the "big flow." There is but one stipulation, you are not allowed to list ranks acquired or years of experience. An example of this might read:

> "I began with a fascination with all thing's martial arts as a child. In my hands every stick was a sword, and every scrap piece of wood was a shield. I built an extensive superhero comic book collection and enjoyed *anime*. As a result, I've trained in defensive tactics as well as classical martial arts. I became a police officer. I chose this profession with the highest goal of martial arts and police work, being of service to my community in the field and on the mat."

Once you have finished the big flow, get a 3x5 card. Write down the three items that constitute who you are as a martial artist. This card will become your guide for the entire writing process. Reducing the example above down to three points we get:

⇨ Lifelong study
⇨ Service

You'll notice that in this instance there are only two points and that is perfect. Two points is fine, one is too few, but never exceed three. That may sound a bit like a Monty Python sketch, but it's important. Your book gets written through this lens.

Your voice can be clinical, as we said previously, or it can be conversational. Either way, you need to unfailingly adhere to your authentic voice. In this fashion you will be more successful in unleashing your creativity without engaging in parroting or plagiarism.

Ted Templeman who produced many successful musicians in the '70s, bands like Van Halen, The Doobie Brothers, Carly Simon, Eric Clapton, Cheap Trick, and Joan Jett, had this to say about music (we paraphrase the quote), "Be identifiable in the first few notes."

This applies just as much to books as it does to music. You have a voice; it is unique. Use it. Your voice is on that 3x5 card, refer to it often as you write.

Know Your Audience

"Having a story is what people connect with, but the story alone doesn't allow you to achieve greatness and results. It's the day-to-day consistency of providing value to your audience."

— Lewis Howes

You know who you are speaking to day in and day out, why is this different?

Know Who You're Speaking To

Once you've found your voice, you need someone to speak to who's interested in hearing what you have to say. It's important to know your audience but be careful not to pander to them. Fresh perspective, backed up with facts and data, is far more saleable than regurgitation of other people's ideas no matter how well-written.

Musashi's Dokkodo takes the Sword Saint's 21 precepts, a mere 21 lines that you can find online for free, and provides five different interpretations of each passage, written from the perspective of lifelong martial artists. In this fashion readers are not buying a simple translation of Musashi's writing, they are scrutinizing his final words for deeper meaning, a fact which makes it a very popular book.

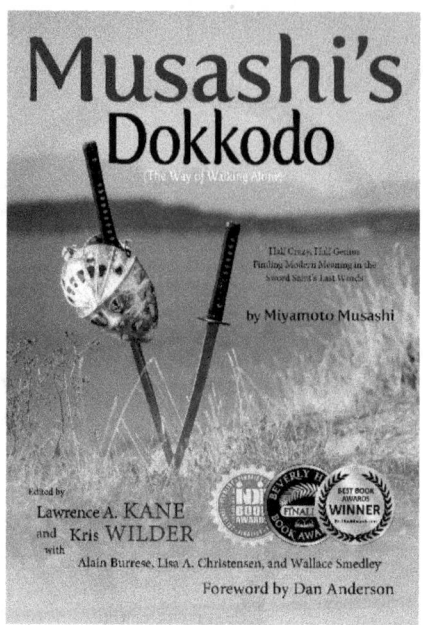

Stay in Your Lane

We primarily write about martial arts, self-defense, and violence in society. Since we're both classically trained martial artists, we tend to use our karate style, *Goju Ryu*, as the lens to focus our perspective regardless of whether we're penning fiction or non-fiction. But, *Goju Ryu* is a small subset of karate which, in turn, is a small subset of martial arts. So, we find topics that appeal as broadly as possible while staying without our sphere of expertise.

That sphere is both broad and eclectic. Kris is not only a Hall of Fame martial artist, but also a Nationally Board-Certified Life Coach. A former member of The Order of St. Francis, he also spent 15 years working as a political advisor. Lawrence, on the other hand, worked stadium security for 26 years where he was directly involved in over 300 violent altercations, which gives a whole new level of meeting to what we learn in the *dojo*. And he's a procurement Hall of Fame member and frequent keynote speaker at sourcing industry conferences.

So, we can speak intelligently to business, leadership, mentoring, coaching, and a wide variety of topics beyond martial arts, though we're careful to not stray so far that we dilute our brand. Our readership expects certain things and looks for our work in certain categories. Brand extension is fine, but straying too far can be problematic. Your audience won't be able to find you—or you'll have to build a new one—and starting over is much harder than incrementally adding to what you already have.

For example, we're primarily known for our non-fiction martial arts books, so when we decided to write a novel, we stuck close to our core subject matter. Our critically acclaimed book *Uma: Champion of the Seven Dojo* has been very well received amongst the martial arts community and beyond, and frequently ranks #1 in karate on Amazon.

What are you great at? What knowledge, skill, and experience do you possess that folks in your sphere of influence want to know more about? Oftentimes it's the things that come easy for you, the natural stuff you barely think about, that's your superpower. If you can coalesce that into actionable advice you've struck gold. Do your research. Know where your sales are likely to come from and target accordingly.

Analytics, Sort Of

Here's an example of our readership:

- ⇨ 75% of readers in the US prefer print books over e-books and audiobooks, and our sales reflect this trend (74.9% print, 19.2% e-book, 5.9% audiobook)
- ⇨ Our readership is 78.2% male and 21.8% female[8]
- ⇨ Customers are predominantly between the ages of 25 and 54
- ⇨ Our most successful marketplaces (in order of sales) include the United States, United Kingdom, Germany, France, Japan, Canada, Italy, Spain, India, Netherlands, and Australia

There is no single dashboard for everything you'll want or need, so you will have to get creative to find information from multiple sources using a variety of methods. Pull from social media, email subscription lists, website data, subscriptions, and similar sources of information to identify and connect with your readership.

You can't write to everyone, so the better you articulate your audience and target their needs the more successful you will be. This process begins with your manuscript and extends through every aspect of publishing, publicity, and sales.

Publishers, including both traditional publishing houses and print-on-demand publishers like KDP, don't collect let alone provide to their talent all the information you'll want so you will discover gaps. Nevertheless, if you know your

---

8   Gender data is currently only available for male and female. There is no sales information we can find that recognizes readers who identify as transgender, gender neutral, non-binary, or other gender identities, so if that's your target audience you'll need to make assumptions on how best to reach them.

audience you can target accordingly. If not, you will almost certainly waste your time and money.

Consider digital marketing by way of example. According to Statista, the most used social media by age range includes:

- 18- to 29-year-olds – Snapchat (41%), TikTok (35%), Instagram (32%)
- 30- to 39-year-olds – LinkedIn (34%), X/Twitter (34%), Snapchat (33%), Instagram (32%)
- 40- to 49-year-olds – LinkedIn (25%), Facebook (22%), X/Twitter (21%)
- 50- to 59-year-olds – Facebook (29%), LinkedIn (24%), Pinterest (24%)

Our readers are largely males between the ages of 25 and 54. Folks in that demographic use Facebook, X/Twitter, YouTube, and LinkedIn, so we don't target Snapchat, Instagram, TikTok, or other sources when trying to connect with them. Where do your potential readers hang out? Armed with that knowledge you can take a pulse of what's urgent and imperative for them, what topics hold their interest, and where they like to spend their money.

Baking Your Book

There's a concept in marketing called "baking cupcakes." The idea is to create small, inexpensive products that you can market test before going all in and baking your proverbial cake. Articles, podcasts, speeches, seminars, and the like allow you to test small ideas and determine what resonates before investing your time, energy, and resources in something bigger. Give it a try.

Word Count

"Three carefully stringed words are worth more than a book of gibberish. It's not the word count but the impact of those words that counts."

— Richelle E. Goodrich

One little nuke is enough, you don't need to kill the world 20,000 times over.

Industry Definitions

While there are no hard-and-fast rules, the book industry publishes definitions of books based on their length. Here's the list:

- Micro-fiction (~ 5 to 350 words)
- Children's picture book (~ 400 to 800 words)
- Flash fiction (~ 500 to 1,000 words)
- Short Stories (~ 1,500 to 5,000 words)
- Novella (~ 10,000 to 50,000 words)
- Middle grade fiction (~ 20,000 to 55,000 words)
- Devotional nonfiction (~ 30,000 to 50,000 words)
- Self-help nonfiction (~ 40,000 to 90,000 words)
- Young adult novel (~ 50,000 to 80,000 words)
- Memoir (~ 50,000 to 90,000 words)
- Narrative nonfiction (~ 50,000 to 110,000 words)
- Adult novel (~ 50,000 to 120,000 words)
- Biography (~ 50,000 to 120,000 words)

For Most, Smaller is Better

A challenge is that, definitional ranges aside, today's audience is largely short attention-span theater. Back when we started writing longer was definitively better, but that's changed rather substantially over the last decade or so. For example, we had a negative review of *The Little Black Book of Violence* on Amazon because the reader thought it was too long. Because of our sense of humor, the sequel, *The Big Bloody Book of Violence*, has a larger word count but shorter page length, so the "little" book is bigger than the "big" book.

Longer books not only have less bang for the proverbial buck since they take longer to get into the marketplace, but they also drive reduced royalties due to higher publishing costs, even in e-book or audiobook format. This has driven a trend of authors writing multiple smaller books rather than fewer bigger ones, and we believe that's a good thing for the industry. In fact, according to wordsrated.com the average length of a NYT bestseller has decreased by 11.8% over the last decade. At the same time, the overall number of long books (over 400 pages) produced was reduced by 30%.

To set yourself up for success, target an audience who's willing to pay and then create value for them. Outline extensively, write in 15-minute (or longer) increments, and stay focused. Steady progress is imperative. You'll likely write your first book seven to twelve times, including your first draft and subsequent iterations.

For most aspiring authors that first draft is the most challenging. After that it becomes easier and easier to polish. So, your number one job is to get the job done. Don't wordsmith as you go. Good, bad, or mediocre, just finish the damn thing. Then you can continuously improve it until it's good enough to go.

Word Count, Smerd Count

This theme is going to come up many times because it is important. The idea of working to a realistic goal, 500 words a day, 250 words a day, it's all good. And nobody cares. Seriously, nobody cares.

No one cares that you have written 20,000 words and you think you've got another 40,000 to go. Some programs and courses recommend that you share your word count because it's going to create excitement with your fan base. That's a falsehood. There is no fan base. A fan base is developed from the product, not the other way around. A simple test is to answer this three-point question, does your sharing educate, inspire, or entertain? If not, it falls flat.

Readers are like mountain sheep ewes, "You rams go butt your heads together, and when you are done come see us." The Ewes don't care. The readers don't care. Think of any successful author, one you like. Have they ever posted a step-by-step accounting of their process? Posting about your process is an amateur move.

The painting, The Mona Lisa, is only 30 inches by 20 inches, give or take. You know who painted it. In 1969 a modern art artist wrapped the coastline of an entire island in pink plastic. Wrapping an island is a massive project, but we're willing to bet you don't know his name. Size and volume have little to do with quality.

Write your story. Write it well. Don't worry about the word count and do not share it with others. It is like trying to teach a pig to sing, it annoys the pig, and it wastes your time.

Just get it done.

Preparation

> "Give me six hours to chop down
> a tree and I will spend the first
> four sharpening the axe."
>
> — Abraham Lincoln

In martial arts you are disciplined, you prepare. Use this for your book too.

Overcoming Fear

Everybody has fears. Most martial artists have confronted small, incremental fears earning rank through the belt system. Even the initial act of walking through the door to go into a martial arts school has anxiety attached to it.

The idea of overcoming fears is more about understanding what lies ahead. The unknown generates an ambient sense of fear. You say to yourself, "I've never written a book. The most I've ever done is a paper I wrote for school." Yeah, being a newbie certainly can bring anxiety, but who cares. Everyone starts someplace.

Miyamoto Musashi wrote in *Go Rin No Sho*, his famous *Book of Five Rings*, that everything is difficult when you first begin. His exact quote, "It may seem difficult at first, but all things are difficult at first."

Welcome to trying something new. Let's set those fears aside, your anxiety to be more precise, and get started. One of the ways to remove anxiety is to understand what's happening and chart a course. In this case, what you need to do is build a structure, a construct in which you can develop your story.

The Process

One of the best references on this process we've ever found is *Save The Cat! The Last Book on Screenwriting You'll Ever Need*, which was published by Blake Snyder in 2005 and remains the number one bestseller in screenwriting today. *Save The Cat!* is about screenwriting, yet it is applicable in many ways to whatever your book is about as long as you are not planning to write a full-on technical manual, what we call a "Make-a-Fist Book" book, which won't sell anyway. More on that later...

David Lynch's movies have grossed over $235 million worldwide. When writing and developing his films he had a method of using file cards to stay on track. He taped file cards on the wall, we believe his magic number was 72 cards, each one describing what would happen throughout the movie in chronological order. In that fashion, he knew with certainty, using short descriptions, exactly what would happen in each scene. This assured both continuity and comprehensiveness. At the end of that, he had a movie. *Save The Cat!* is more structured but utilizes a similar concept for staying on track.

Which of these two methods, Lynch's file cards or Blake Snyder's approach, do we recommend? Well, we have used both. These formats are tools. Tools need to fit the job. We will say this, *Save The Cat!* is transferable to most formats and has a tight structure. David Lynch's method is not as tight, and that can result in some frustration, but it adds more flexibility.

Having an entire *dojo* wall covered with butcher paper and sticky notes (our more modern version of file cards) is fun. The nice thing about sticky notes is that they're easy to move around as your ideas play out. An entire weekend of coffee, colored markers, and scribbling on a wall is what set us up for success with numerous books. You can do a virtual version of that with modern technology too, but there's a connection between handwriting and creative thought that tends to get lost over Slack, Webex, Teams, or whichever platform you choose.

Preparation over Perspiration

We suggest you approach the layout of your book in the same way you would do when planning to paint a room. Sure, you could go buy some paint, slap it on the wall, and get it done, but that usually doesn't work very well. Professional painters spend more time preparing to paint than they do painting.

Professionals use Trisodium Phosphate (TSP) to wash the walls before they get started, removing oils and other debris that might blemish the finish. Then they apply painter's tape, masking off all areas they're not planning to paint. Finally, the floor gets covered with a drop cloth.

Once all that preparation is done, then they apply the coating, usually starting with primer and once that's dry using paint. The last step, the actual painting, takes moments in skilled hands. If you break a painting project into these steps, you can see the preparation takes more effort than the painting.

The same thing applies to writing a book. Some books, such as *Dude, The World's Gonna Punch You in the Face*, take far, far longer to research and lay out than they do writing. In that case, we had to figure out how to get teenagers to accept advice without their parents or guardians forcing it on them, which led to a salacious, attention-grabbing cover and an interior flow that could be read in virtually any page order with actionable takeaways in every section.

Our beta testing started with an adult leaving the book out, say on the coffee table or back of the toilet where it would be found that their teen. They all reported back that when first spotted, the teen would pick up the book, glance at the cover, and set it back down. On the second pass, he'd pick it up, flip it over, and peek at the back cover. The third time the teen would flip the book open to a random page and give it a quick read. Shortly thereafter the book would disappear for a month or so, and the teen would suddenly become a better person. That's exactly what we were hoping for, but it took precise engineering from start to finish to get to that point.

As you can see, writing is like painting. Take time to organize your thoughts, preparing the "canvas" for your words. Lay things out in clear, understandable sections, outline the hell out of it, and then begin writing.

Preparation, preparation, preparation. Whether it is reading the book *Save The Cat!* and taking Blake Snyder's advice or taping file cards or sticky notes up on the wall in your office, prepare. Writing is smoother and far more enjoyable when you have a goal and direction. Just like a good kick, where biomechanics help you hit the target, preparation will assure you succeed.

Create Compelling Value

"Try not to become a man of success.
Rather become a man of value."

— Albert Einstein

**Write the book you'd
pay to read.**

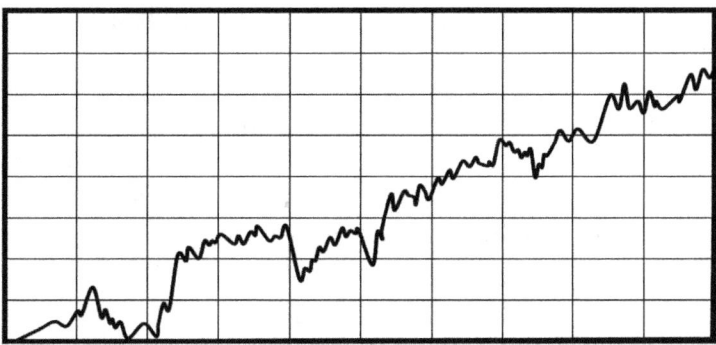

Five Questions of Value

Dave Grohl once wrote, "Always have the highest bar for yourself. Wake up every day and no matter how crappy you feel, want to change something for the better. Do something that makes someone happy. Create something that inspires someone. Be someone's light when they are hopeless."

That quote really speaks to value, doesn't it? In that same fashion, your book should inspire, entertain, and make someone's day. So, what are you planning to write? And, how do you know that readers will value it. A good way to know is to ask yourself five questions:

- ⇨ Who is this book about?
- ⇨ What do they want?
- ⇨ Why can't they get it?
- ⇨ What do they do about it?
- ⇨ Why doesn't it work?

We'll walk through each in turn...

Who is The Book About?

If it is you, you should rethink what you are about to do. The reason is nobody cares. Nobody will want to own your book. It's your struggle and everybody has their own challenges they face daily. They don't need to hear about how hard you had it.

"Fans" is an abbreviation of the word "fanatic," a person of unreasoning and extreme enthusiasm. Taylor Swift enthusiasts are fanatics. They will happily shell out $7,000 or more for tickets to her concerts. In fact, first-night tickets for her sold-out shows at SoFi Stadium in Inglewood California sold for as much as $11,000 on StubHub in 2023. They will download any song she produces, buy her t-shirts and posters, scoop up ghostwritten Taylor Swift biographies, and more.

Taylor Swift fans are also the same people who have no idea who Vespasian was. They don't know or care how Vespasian (9 AD - 79 AD) rose from humble birth as the son of a mule-herder to become Rome's emperor after the civil wars that followed Nero's death. They couldn't care less about how he led fiscal reforms that stabilized the empire or the impact his actions had on the world.

You're not Taylor Swift... and you're not Vespasian. Now if you want to leave some information for your family and a few close friends, go ahead. Perhaps a handful of people will read it.

Never forget, however, that Bruce Lee's best-selling book isn't about him, it is about his methods. Those methods you can use. Any martial artist can. They are valuable. Similarly, you can use your personal story to impart important lessons for others, but make the book about them, not about you.

What Do They Want?

Readers want the secret keys to the proverbial magic kingdom. It is human nature. The lust after shortcuts, easy ways to succeed. This desire is evident in almost every ad on social media, with pitches like, 'The 10 mistakes you can't afford to make." Insert any title that touches on fear of loss, or the promise of easy gains and the reader's limbic system gets ignited.

Kris has a friend of some 50 years who owns a large car dealership. Kris asked him, "What is the key to selling a car?" His friend replied, "Most people think they know what they want, but they don't. Once I find out what they really want I get it for them." He went on to explain, "The research they bring into the dealership tells me what they desire. They think they are armed with information, and they are, but it's not what they think. Their information tells me what is important to them, what they desire."

This is reminiscent of Henry Ford's famous quote about innovation, "If I had asked people what they wanted, they would have said faster horses." That leaves you with a conundrum. If people are inclined to tell you what they want, then you should ask them what they desire, right? Wrong.

An Award-Winning Mistake, of Sorts

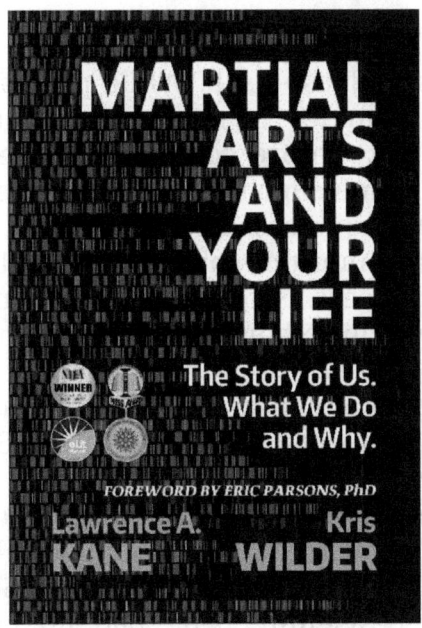

One of the best, most award-winning books we ever wrote, *Martial Arts and Your Life*, is dead. It doesn't sell. Before we wrote that dead book, we went to our mailing list and social media. We asked, "We are thinking about writing this book, what do you think?" The answers were:

"Absolutely!"

"That sounds interesting."

"100%"

"Do it."

It's an Eric Hoffer Award nominated, Living Now Book Awards Gold Medalist, eLit Book Awards Gold Medalist, National Indie Excellence Award winner, Independent Press Award winner, Global Book Awards Silver Medalist, San Francisco Book Festival honorable mention, New York Book Festival honorable mention, and American Book Fest Best Book Awards finalist, but it doesn't sell.

Did the folks we asked lie to us? No. We're certain those responses were well-intentioned and honest. Like customers at the car dealership, they thought they knew what they wanted... but they didn't.

After that initial contact we followed up, "Would you participate?"

"Yes!" again.

Nevertheless, it doesn't sell. While participation by some elite performers carries the book, most readers simply don't care. If you think we are complaining, we're not. We are sharing a simple message with you. Folks really don't know what they want, so success comes from a combination of market research, intuition, and luck. In other words, your best shot for success is to write from your heart, create something useful for others, and do your best to make sure they find out about it.

In the early days of podcasting, Lawrence did an interview with Dr. Helen that went viral, generating 28,000 book sales in a single month. Conversely, Kris was interviewed on Howard Stern's show, and it did nothing for sales. Connecting with the right audience is paramount. Dr. Helen's listeners cared about the material whereas Howard Stern's did not.

Our current bestselling book had no market research before publishing. We just thought it would be an interesting and thought-provoking concept. Then, it languished for a few years before it exploded in sales. And we honestly don't know why. It suddenly bloomed.

So, do your homework, and recognize your audience, but understand that they don't necessarily know what they want. Not really. You'll need to intuit their desire. We'll tease out how to do that throughout the rest of this chapter...

Why Can't They Get It?

You might think you have come up with the best thing since sliced bread, but what unmet need does your idea resolve for prospective readers? What value does it create? And, importantly, what do you offer that they cannot get from someone else?

Make your book useful to others. The fastest way to do that is to create a simple outline providing a solution to a problem that will resonate with likely readers. Here is a sample we recommend:

- Introduce the topic
- Identify the problem
- Explain the cause of the problem
- Address the reader's reaction
- Describe the main takeaway (how the problem is solved)
- Explain why it's solved
- Provide actionable items that readers can use
- End

This format works for almost all styles of writing. It helps you solve problems. It helps assure you're creating value. Think of every person you find interesting, every story, every show you enjoy. These people, stories, and shows have some form of resolution. The most satisfying takeaways are the ones that answer a question folks deeply care about or are intrigued by. Here are a few examples:

- Why do we train the way we train?
- What are the rewards for martial arts training?
- Can I have a hero's journey too?
- What is the best way to teach martial arts in a school system?

⇨ What must I do to be successful without becoming a *McDojo*?
⇨ Can this fictional story both entertain and inform me?

According to a recent Gallup poll, despite ever increasing access to social media, online games, movies, gambling, and other sources of entertainment, most Americans still enjoy reading books. Here are some of their findings:

⇨ 39% of people surveyed read more than 10 books a year
⇨ 91% of people surveyed read at least one book a year
⇨ The ten bestselling fiction categories include (in order) mystery/suspense, general fiction, romance, thrillers, Christian fiction, women's fiction, historical fiction, young adult, literary fiction, and science fiction/fantasy
⇨ The ten bestselling non-fiction categories include (in order) cooking, medicine/health, biography/memoir[9], arts/crafts/collectibles, history, how to, self-help/psychology, travel, current events/political, and religion/philosophy

The good news is that people still read, but the bad news is that you won't find martial arts prominent on the list of top categories they like. For non-fiction martial arts are a subset of sports/outdoors, whereas for fiction they can fit into multiple different categories, including historical fiction, young adult, and general fiction. So, while you're not aiming at the broadest possible audience, the good news is that sometimes it's easier to stand out in a niche crowd. It's a big fish, small pond sort of thing. You can do that by guiding readers on how to get from here to there, showing them the way.

Word of mouth is your best advertising, so when you create value and readers tell their friends who enjoy your work and tell their friends in turn suddenly you have a

---

9 Of famous people not everyday citizens. Examples include folks like Albert Einstein, Anthony Bourdain, Dave Grohl, Elie Wiesel, Elizabeth Wurtzel, Malala Yousafzai, Maya Angelou, Michelle Obama, Norm MacDonald, Rosa Parks, Steven King, Taylor Swift, Viola Davis, and Winston Churchill.

bestseller. That's almost certainly what happened with our book which blew up sales-wise despite no viral social media posts or other indicators. Word of mouth explains our sudden success. The way that online bookseller algorithms work, once a book starts trending it becomes easier for folks to find, so it's a self-reinforcing cycle.

What Do They Do About It?

If someone chooses to buy your book it will be because they believe you have the answers, the joy, the story. Your book must be meaningful, useful, and relevant for them. But, if they have never heard of you or your work they can't buy it, so you can't just have great content, marketing is paramount. You need to stand out amongst the millions of new titles released every year. According to a recent survey, the top reasons (in rank order) that readers buy books include:

⇨ The author is someone famous
⇨ The book is recommended by a friend, social media influencer, blogger, or online review
⇨ The book is required for work or school
⇨ The book was given as a gift from a friend or colleague
⇨ The book won a prestigious award
⇨ The book is a bestseller
⇨ They have read previous books by the author

As you can see, knowing, liking, and trusting the author, even via surrogates, entices folks to buy. If you're already famous and have a good reputation that's easy, but if you're not you're going to have to social media the living hell out of your work.

If you don't have good content, however, you can waste millions on advertising for very little return.

For example, the more positive reviews a book has on Amazon the higher it will rank in their search results, increasing discoverability. Because of this algorithm, books with an average review over 4.0 sell nearly six times better than ones with reviews that average under 3.0. Further, authors tend to only get reviews on 3% to 5% of their sales, so a high review count tends to indicate a high level of interest, which can also bump up your sales if the average rating is relatively high.

Why Doesn't It Work?

If your book doesn't sell it's either because you didn't answer the question that was being asked or because no one has ever heard of you. It is that simple. But how you answer that question matters, how you let a person know that you have solved their unmet need with your content. We'll cover this more later, but your book's cover and title need to spark enough interest for a potential reader to determine whether it's a good fit. And they must do it with a two-second glance.

A book titled *My Journey in The Martial Arts* sounds like navel-gazing. It's narcissistic and uninteresting to 99.99999% of potential readers. But let's pretend for a moment that you're not a self-absorbed egotist and have something important to say that creates value for a reader. In that case, let's take that book and retitle it. For example, *ADHD and Martial Arts: How Karate Helped Me Conquer Attention-Deficit/Hyperactivity Disorder: And How You Can Do It Too.*

While that's by no means a "perfect" title, among other things it's way too wordy, but it does portray value far, far better than the first one. And it can grab the attention of others looking to solve the same problem.

If you do things right, say making your book available for presale and running a successful social media campaign to attract attention, there's an extra bump you can achieve when your book is first released. Amazon and other sellers not only highlight their bestselling titles but also showcase hot new releases. Being a #1 new release is a great way to build momentum, even for niche books like this one:

Yes, even a book on the anatomical effects of an obscure karate *kata* can sell well if written properly and advertised correctly. The bottom line is that for your book to work it must create value, something of consequence that's obvious to anyone who chooses to pick it up or click on the thumbnail to find out more.

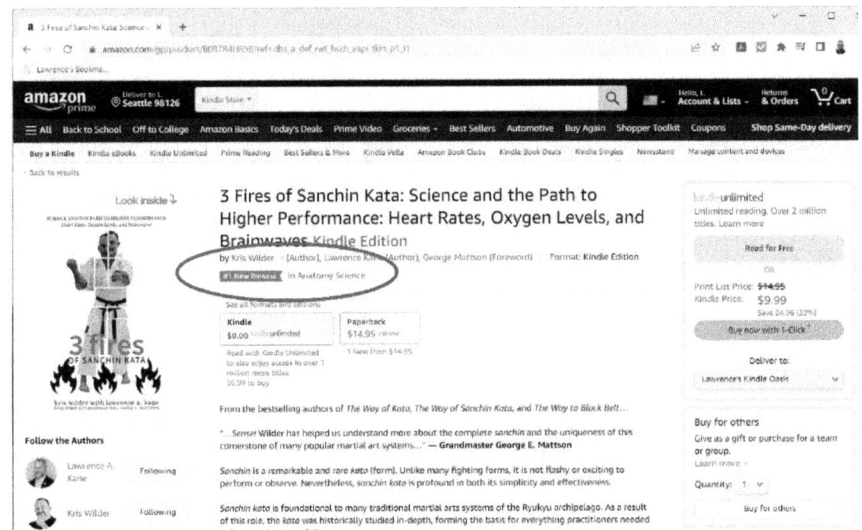

Look at Me, I Wrote a Book!

*"Either write something worth reading
or do something worth writing."*

— Benjamin Franklin

**Nobody cares, except
maybe your mother, and
then only in passing.**

Let's face it, if you write it, they won't come. We've said it before, but it bears repeating, to break through the noise you must social media the living hell out of your book. Know your readership demographics and leverage Facebook, Instagram, LinkedIn, Twitch, Pinterest, Reddit, Snapchat, TikTok, X/Twitter, YouTube, or whichever platform(s) they're most likely to hang out on for digital marketing campaigns. Engage in "guerilla marketing" activities, such as appearing in podcast interviews or writing articles for prestigious periodicals, that grow your footprint and reputation.

No one cares if you write a book. Nobody cares if you write a dozen books. What they care about is what that book is going to do for them. Is the book going to bring them structure? Is the book going to be insightful on a topic that they care about? Is the book going to solve their problem? Is the book going to bring them enjoyment?

The I of The Eye

The biggest problem new authors have in publicizing their work is saying, "I wrote a book!" To begin, you started with the word "I." "I" is a terrible term with which to begin any kind of promotional material. "I" seems narcissistic, hence doesn't do well. It only works with marquee names.

Think of it this way, "Hi, I'm Dwayne 'The Rock' Johnson and I'm here to tell you about a new book I wrote." That is a celebrity promotion. Take out his name and insert yours, and nobody cares. They don't know you. They don't like you. And they don't trust you (in part since they've never heard of you).

If you begin promotional materials with the word "I," you have already failed. You are not serving the needs of your audience. At no time does the audience care about how difficult your book writing journey was. Sure, it's an arduous task, but nobody cares how many hours you spend. The sweat, the effort that you put into making sure that what you wrote was the best book that you could make, it all means nothing unless it is measured in terms of usefulness to the reader.

In other words, it's not the effort that counts, it's the outcome. Think of it this way, if you go to a fancy restaurant and order your steak medium rare, you don't care how many Michelin-Stars the chef may have earned if he or she burns your Wagyu ribeye. You send it back. It's an $840 steak for God's sake, either it's cooked right or you won't eat it.

Focusing on the effort that you're putting in is a common problem for first-time authors. This is natural because writing is an internal process. It is self-guided in structure. The idea is all yours, the effort is all yours, the outcome is on you, and that creates an atmosphere that leads to the use of the word "I." Yes, it's your work, but "I" is not going to sell one book.

A Simple Tactic

Here's a simple tactic that you can use to avoid this error. Make sure every promotional piece that you write, be it an advertisement, blog post, social media blurb, or whatever you choose to compose does not begin with the word "I." Here's an example:

> "I wrote this new spy thriller about a South African special agent running through the Northwest Territories of Canada. He's being chased by the Royal Canadian Mounted Police and a spook known only as the Boer."

Or

> "A South African special agent finds himself in the Northwest Territories of Canada. He needs every skill, every instinct he's honed to evade the Royal Canadian Mounted Police. Plus, a suspicious special operative who has his own agenda."

Take a pause and feel how those two versions sit in your emotional structure. One of them is as dry as Southern Nevada, the other is juicy. Now go look on the web at how many authors make this mistake. And take note, no top-selling author uses the word "I" in their publicity or promotion unless they're already major-league famous.

Know, Like, Trust (KLT)

All marketing for your books should focus on getting readers to think they know you, like you, and trust you. In business that's called the KLT principle; it's used to build strong, long-lasting relationships with clients. For authors it incentivizes them to buy your work, read it, and tell their friends about it.

Word of mouth is your best testimonial when you create value, and your worst enemy when you don't. Consequently, in addition to merely marketing your book, it's valuable to showcase your knowledge through interviews, articles, blog postings, speeches, and other venues. The goal is to become as widely known by potential readers as possible.

Here's an epic line from *Pirates of the Caribbean, The Curse of the Black Pearl*, one that's still celebrated with memes decades after that movie's release:

Norrington: "You are without doubt the worst pirate I've ever heard of!"

Sparrow: "But you have heard of me."

That's the goal, assuring that they have heard of you. And in a good way. Another method of building your brand is through external recognition such as book awards. Here's an example:

Industry Recognition

When one of our books earned the Beverly Hills Book Award's Presidential Prize the prize not only came with cool recognition, a medal, and a digital sticker for our book cover, but also with $12,000 in professional marketing, which was a substantial sum back in 2016. That landed us interviews on a variety of nationally syndicated and local radio shows. For example, spending an hour on the Jim Bohannon show, which was simulcast on over 500 stations nationwide, not only led to an increase in book sales but also got our name out in ways we could never have done without winning that award.

While the Beverly Hills Book Awards no longer exist, there are numerous similar awards worth applying to once your book is published. Here's a short sample:

- ⇨ The Eric Hoffer Book Award (https://www.hofferaward.com/), which celebrates accomplishments of small, academic, and independent press around the world
- ⇨ eLit Awards (https://www.elitawards.com/) which celebrate excellence in digital creation and publishing, including audiobooks, websites, video channels, and podcasts
- ⇨ Foreword Indies (https://www.forewordreviews.com/awards/), which celebrate the most creative, innovative, and beautiful books published through independent press
- ⇨ The Living Now Book Awards (https://www.livingnowawards.com/), which celebrate books that enrich their reader's lives
- ⇨ The National Indie Excellence Awards (https://www.indieexcellence.com/), which celebrate noteworthy accomplishments from independent press and self-publishing
- ⇨ The National Book Foundation Award (https://www.nationalbook.org/), which celebrates the best literature published in the United States
- ⇨ The Pulitzer Prize (https://www.pulitzer.org/), which celebrates fiction and non-fiction works in print, digital, magazine journalism, musical composition, and literature

The above is by no means an all-encompassing list. There are a veritable ton of awards out there covering both large press and independent publishing, including a variety of niche categories like Christian-themed books, children's books, and book design, among others. If you go through a traditional publisher, they'll submit nominations for you whereas if you choose small press or self-publishing you will likely have to do it yourself.

Including the aforementioned Beverly Hills Book Award and Presidential Prize, we have also won a USA Best Books Award, three National Indie Excellence Book Awards, three

Independent Press Awards, a Next Generation Indie Book Award, a NYC Big Book Award, four eLit Gold Medals, and a Living Now Book Awards Gold Medal, along with numerous other writing and publishing honors.

We'll never know for certain how the prestige associated with those awards impacts sales, there's no direct correlation, but we do know that it's impactful. And we get "free" advertising when each contest publishes their winner's list which is always a good thing. Our point isn't to brag, it's to demonstrate the value that this strategy can bring, assuming you create valuable content of course.

You can also purchase professional reviews from reputable outfits like Clarion Review or BlueInk Review, which can be a good idea for first-time writers who haven't built a track record or fanbase yet. Each review is written by one of their qualified experts, handpicked by a managing editor to ensure that they have the requisite knowledge to write credibly about your work.

Librarians and booksellers subscribe to both these services, and they highlight their best finds on social media, so positive reviews can directly drive sales too. If you receive a negative appraisal, you have the option of using it to understand your shortcomings and improve your book accordingly while asking them to not publish it.

While industry recognition is awesome, scrutinize how anything you're planning to apply to works both to avoid intellectual property theft as well as to avoid anything that reeks of pay-for-play as that can backfire by undermining your reputation.

Ask for Forewords and Blurbs

Another way to demonstrate value, especially as a new author, is to have someone more famous or prestigious than you write a foreword to your book. Not only does that add gravitas to your writing, but it also expands your footprint into the other author's sphere of influence. Presumably they'll help chum up your book on social media, they liked it enough to write the foreword after all, but even if they do absolutely nothing anyone who searches for their name when looking to buy books will discover your book.

For example, Lawrence convinced Martial Arts Masters Hall of Fame Member Loren W. Christensen to write the foreword for his book *Surviving Armed Assaults*, which helped turn it into a bestseller. When the 13th most dangerous man in the world as elected by *Black Belt Magazine,* says

nice stuff about your writing it helps tremendously. And Loren is an all-around great guy who remembered those who helped him with his first books and happily paid that goodwill forward.

Surviving Armed Assaults was published by a publisher who requires their authors to solicit testimonials from celebrities to help promote their books, but no matter how you publish you should do the same thing. It reinforces KLT.

In Lawrence's case, he also got back cover "blurbs" from British Combat Association Hall of Fame Members Peter Consterdine and Iain Abernethy, along with retired CIA agent and bestselling author Barry Eisler, Tactical Medical Director of Toledo (Ohio) SWAT Dr. Jeff Cooper, University of Washington Police Chief Vicky Stormo, and Killology Research Group Director Lt. Col. Dave Grossman. That's pretty good "firepower" for an author's third book, demonstrating the value of its content, and helping it garner worldwide attention.

Our point—if you don't ask the answer will always be "no." So, once your manuscript is ready to go, reach out to folks whose work you used in your bibliography or whose books you enjoy and request that they do you a solid by writing a foreword or blurb. Chances are good that if your writing is valuable, they'll say yes.

Abandon The "Make-a-Fist Book"

"You feel like if they just read the manual first... If we had a manual, that is."

— Jeff VanderMeer

In today's world everyone thinks they know. Whether they do or don't, they know they do.

The Golden Rule

"I should start at the beginning." This is a common place for the author to start, it only makes sense. At the beginning is how you learned martial arts too. When it comes to martial arts publications this is what we call a "Make-a-Fist Book." The challenge is that a Make-a-Fist Book is not a book, it's a manual. If it sounds like we are condescending towards the Make-a-Fist Book, we are. Manuals are fine. Manuals have a purpose. But, They're not books.

How do you know the difference? Generally, books are not helpful in application whereas manuals are. Think of it in the same way you might consider the Golden Rule. The Golden Rule is the principle of treating others as you would want them to treat you. It describes the ethics of reciprocity, a useful principle.

It is difficult if not impossible to break that rule down into line-item actions that contain every possible context you might encounter, however. You see, the Golden Rule is a moving target governed by an overarching principle. You apply it to any given situation strategically not tactically. Martial arts are much the same way. A static picture of a response to a head punch is minimally helpful as the real-world answer is, "It depends."

Is the punch part of a drill or an actual attack? Are you facing social or a-social violence? Is the aggressor intoxicated? Is he alone or does he have friends who might join in the fray? Are they angry? Are you with friends who might intervene? Did you do something to warrant the attack? Is the aggressor larger or smaller than you, more or less fit, physically stronger or weaker? How far away are they? Are you injured, disabled, mentally or physically compromised in some way that impacts how you might receive the attack? Are there witnesses you can turn to for help? Is the incident recorded on video? Etc., etc., the list goes on and on.

You get the idea... the "textbook" answer only works under certain, constrained, very limited circumstances. It's static, of limited fidelity. Consequently, this line-item act belongs in a manual not in a book. Frankly, the world does not need another Make-a-Fist Book. If you want to know how to make a fist you can find thousands of YouTube videos, instruction manuals, and references. Or you can go ask your *sensei*.

You're not a Beginner, Write a Real Book

How many times have you picked up a martial arts book or opened an electronic sample and the first thing you find yourself looking at is something about how you stand in a particular stance? This is one of many examples of the Make-a-Fist Book. Don't forget what Gichin Funakoshi, founder of *Shotokan* karate, wrote, "Stances are for beginners."

He's right, of course, but his statement is more profound than it may seem at face value. Think of it this way: If you're writing a book about something, you're not a beginner. Why then should your work be written for beginners? Don't target beginners with your book, give juice, give value beyond mundane expectations.

A manual is only good for those in close association. If you choose to write a manual God bless you, carry on. It is useful to your group, organization, or tribe. If you choose to write a real book, on the other hand, you must bring larger value to an audience far beyond those in your inner circle. That's the stuff that will sell, for which readers will want to own and happily pay.

Follow these guidelines and avoid writing the Make-a-Fist Book. Focus on what your audience will want to own, read, and refer to repeatedly. Discard the rest. That's how you assure value.

Setting a Writing Schedule

> "People who succeed have momentum. The more they succeed, the more they want to succeed, and the more they find a way to succeed."
>
> — Tony Robbins

Newborns need routine. Treat your manuscript like the baby it is.

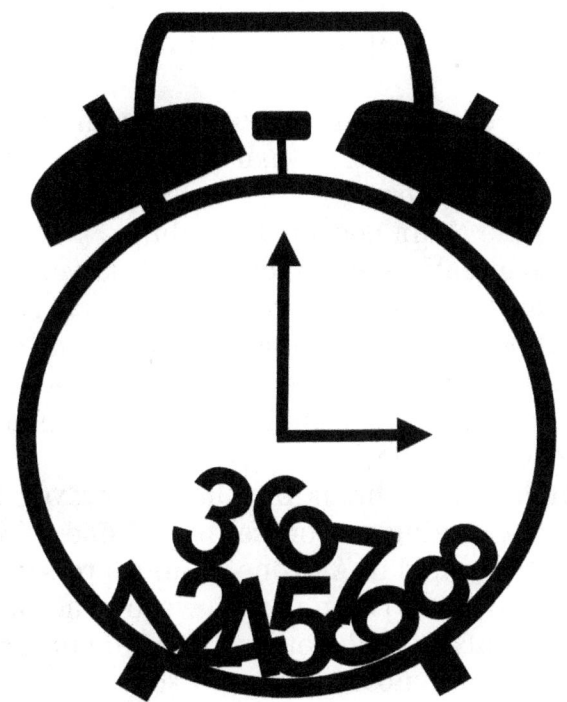

We're Creatures of Habit

For better or worse, we are all creatures of habit. For instance, if someone hasn't been back to their martial arts class for two weeks after taking a break from training, the likelihood of them returning is low. You've seen it happen, a diligent student receives an injury, takes a vacation, travels on business, or whatever, and afterward you never see them again.

If you don't contact them their schedule changes and their world will move on. That student is no longer going to be attending class. They drift away. We can argue why, how, and what the cause was, but the point is that it doesn't take long to create a habit, in this case a habit of failure.

Habit makes the difference when you're keeping your writing schedule. Comedian Jerry Seinfeld had a great way of going about writing his comedy act and TV show. What he did was simple, he made an "X" on the calendar every day he wrote. Seinfeld's goal was to not break the chain. Don't break the chain.

Seinfeld didn't say how much he was going to write. He didn't mandate 500 words, it wasn't going to be 1,500 words, he was simply going to write. He refused to break the chain. Not breaking the chain became his habit.

We want to create a habit of the book you're writing becoming paramount in your mind. The book is the thing that must happen. If your writing schedule is just 15 minutes a day, so be it. Our recommendation is the same as Jerry Seinfeld's, don't break the chain. Even if it's one singular sentence, write every day.

Now a confession, we break the chain. However, we are so maniacal about staying on course that whenever we do we double down the next day. And one of our secrets is that most of our projects are co-written so we have joint accountability, neither of us wants to let the other down. You probably don't have that luxury as most writers go solo. To be clear this pressure is not a burden, it is a luxury, and we embrace it for success. Whether you're writing solo or in tandem, adopt a habit of writing.

Everybody is Writing a Book

Many people have a book that they're writing. We have one mutual friend who's been writing a book for 20 years. Yes, 20 years! When was the last time she pulled that document out and wrote it? We no longer bother to ask...

Everybody is writing a book. Yes, that is an exaggeration, a slight one, but once it is discovered you are working on a book these writers will come out of the woodwork. They're happy to share their journey of incompleteness.

Everybody has an idea for a screenplay, a book, a movie, a Netflix series. As harsh as this sounds, virtually none of these people have a habit of achievement. That's why a mere 1.8% of aspiring writers get published.[10]

If you can write, you write. If you can take a note, you take that note. If you can't take a note, you can keep an idea in mind until you can jot it down. It's that simple. Be obligated, be prepared. Keith Richards of the *Rolling Stones* got the idea for Jumping Jack Flash in his sleep, woke, captured that idea, and made rock-n-roll history. It's amazing what your subconscious can do, even when you're focused on other things, once you've inculcated a habit of content creation.

Be a Monomaniac

Establish your time and what your writing environment is going to look like. Everybody has their way of going about it. There's no hard-and-fast rule, but here are a few suggestions: First off put your phone in another room, you don't need the distraction. It's only going to create a cloudy world.

Kris only answers the phone if it is a call from a few key people whose ringtone he's preset. Kris' room is silent when he writes. If he's writing that's it, he's writing. There is a window of creativity in his world, the moment he starts his window is seen as closing. That's all he's doing writing. Oh, and he uses drugs too, coffee.

Lawrence does something similar. He has a computer desk and laptop set aside for nothing but research and writing. He puts on a set of noise-canceling headphones, cranks up the tunes to block out other distractions, and loses himself in his work. And yeah, his phone is muted for the duration of his writing. He's addicted to caffeine too, so there's always coffee involved.

You can find whatever it is that makes for your environment for writing work for you. Some people use white noise, jazz music in the background, or utter silence. You likely have some idea of what works in your world. Use it. Once you've latched on to what it is you need to have for your

---

10 That statistic includes traditional press, niche, and self-publishing, so back in the days before print-on-demand it would have been even less.

environment, your method, and your means of creation, keep it and use it. When you do, your brain knows you're in writing mode and will unleash your creative juices. Become a creature of habit.

This habit will help create effective time usage. You will get more out of whatever interval you have available to write. If you want to set a target, go ahead, it's the way that you work. The most important thing to do is to continuously make progress, not to become that student who has sluffed away from the *dojo* after two weeks off never to be seen again. Or that person who has been "working" on their book for 20 years.

To paraphrase Tony Robbins, people who have momentum succeed.

Going it Alone Creates Inferior Product

For most authors it's easier to edit than it is to create, so maintain your momentum by getting words out of your head and onto your laptop, tablet, or whatever it is you write with as quickly as possible before worrying about using the perfect words and sentence structure to communicate your ideas. If you go through a mainstream publisher, they will provide an editor (several actually), whereas if you self-publish you can hire one, but either way don't let the pursuit of perfection be the enemy of the good.

Once you've got a solid first draft you can worry about editing, tweaking content, assuring clarity, and polishing away the fluff. For example, most first-time writers have a bad case of adverb poisoning, especially in fiction books. As Stephen King wrote, "The road to hell is paved with adverbs." Adverbs add to word count but rarely add value for the reader.

The first few iterations you'll want to do yourself, but you'll need to hire professionals to help with your first book.[11] So, once you're satisfied with your manuscript work with editors to polish it up.

11   Even if your publisher provides editors, the better your submission draft the higher the likelihood they'll be willing to sign a contract and produce it.

There are multiple different types of editors. Start with developmental, substantive, or content editing, leveraging a professional to help assure a valid layout and optimal flow for your work. They ensure you're both meeting your readers' needs as well as producing the right level of content, not too much or too little.

Next, you'll probably want a fact checker, someone to pour through your manuscript looking for errors. It's critical for non-fiction, but even novels can benefit from fact-checking. Oftentimes that's more challenging that you might imagine, and in most book contracts, it is the writer's legal responsibility not their publisher's, to deliver a factually accurate text. Even if you don't get sued, if you get something wrong the scandal can undermine your reputation.

Once you have a polished manuscript, you'll move on to copy editing, tightening up the content, before having a proofreader look for grammatical or spelling errors that are easy to miss when you know what you think you've written hence missing what's on the page.

Those are not the only types of editors, others include acquisition editors, line editors, beta readers, etc., and they all have unique skills and perspectives. Unless you're going through one of the Big Five publishers, you're not likely to need or use all of them, but the key is to ensure you have a well-written, clear, and comprehensive work before it's published.

No one is good at everything, so don't be afraid to pay someone, or multiple people, to assure first-time quality. It's worth the investment.

"Writer's Block" is for Losers

"Don't stop because you've hit a block. Finish the page, even if you write nothing but your own name. The block will break if you don't give in to it. Remember, writing is a physical habit as well as whatever you want to think it is—calling, avocation, talent, genius, art."

— Isabelle Holland

You self-indulgent little whelp.

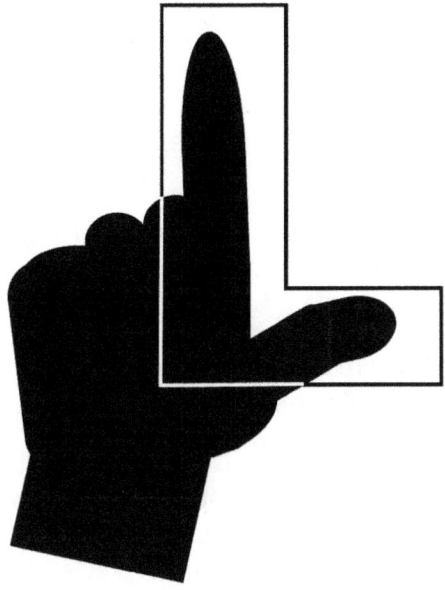

Writer's block is a bunch of bullshit conjured up by self-indulgent faux artists to create a unique burden that they can share with others to publicly prove how special they are. No one cares one whit about your burden of creativity. They have bills to pay, jobs to do, and a wild mosaic of problems to resolve you likely haven't seen. Your contrived writer's block is not on their radar of care.

You didn't get to the place you are in martial arts by saying, "I'm just not feeling it tonight." You won't get a book published by whining about how hard it is. As we've already said, don't complain.

According to a recent article from the Graduate School of Biomedical Sciences at UT Health San Antonio, the real cause of so-called writer's block stems from a combination of one or more of the following factors: fear of failure, fear of success, boredom, perfectionism, and self-sabotage. It can also be exacerbated by running out of meaningful things to say about a particular subject or genre. Notice that there's no neuroscience attributed to any of those reasons.

We could rant more, but in the spirit of brevity we'll leave you with a scene from the cult classic *Office Space*. In that film there is a scene where Peter speaks to his neighbor Lawrence about the differences in their work environments. Peter works in an office whereas Lawrence works on a construction site:

> Peter: "When you come in on Monday and you're not feeling well, does anyone ever say to you, 'Sounds like somebody's got a case of the Mondays?'"
>
> Lawrence: "No. No man, shit no. I believe you'd get your ass kicked saying something like that."

Pretty much sums it up, doesn't it? If you have taken our suggestion and outlined your work extensively, it's easy to dive into whatever section works for you at any given moment. There's no excuse for writer's block.

Don't be a loser, write!

Jeweler's Loop Reviews

"Perfectionism is the voice of the oppressor, the enemy of the people. It will keep you cramped and insane your whole life, and it is the main obstacle between you and a shitty first draft. I think perfectionism is based on the obsessive belief that if you run carefully enough, hitting each stepping-stone just right, you won't have to die. The truth is that you will die anyway and that a lot of people who aren't even looking at their feet are going to do a whole lot better than you, and have a lot more fun while they're doing it."

— Anne Lamott

Ignore the negativity and move on, you're a maker not a taker.

Errors are Inevitable

W. Somerset Maugham (1874 - 1965) was a writer from England who was born in Paris and educated at a German university. He wrote plays, short stories, and novels. Several of his works were adapted into film. Maugham was a Fellow of the Royal Society of Literature. He was also a Fellow of the Library of Congress, an honorary member of the American Academy of Arts and Letters, and an honorary senator of Heidelberg University. He was a guy who clearly knew how to write, and was good at his job, yet the 3rd edition of his book, *The Razors Edge*, contains a typo.

Our point: You are going to have an error in your book. This is not a "get-out-of-jail-free" card, but it is an understanding that it's going to happen and you will get called out for it.

You must do your best to avoid, to correct, and to edit, but errors are going to happen, even with professional editing and proofreading.

One of our books was edited both by us and someone we hired before being submitted to the publisher. After we signed the contract, it was copy edited, line edited, beta tested, and proofread multiple times by experienced professionals. When we received our proof copy to validate in the mail and flipped it open, Lawrence found a typo on the first page he turned to. After it was published, Kris found another one.

Some people who have never taken up the arduous task of writing or editing a book are going to strap on the jeweler's loop and scrutinize your work. These people have one intent, to find an error. That's what they live for.

Basement-Dwelling Troglodytes

This jeweler-loop nitpicking is a faux-empowering act. And there are a lot of folks out there who will proudly put whatever they find wrong in their review. They will often begin with, "That being said...," or "However..." This dynamic is okay, assuming you take the criticism as an opportunity to sharpen your sword and not as a personal attack. It isn't personal; they're basement-dwellers who are trying to make themselves feel better about their otherwise mundane lives. It has nothing to do with you.

Many authors don't bother reading reviews of their work. We do, but we also know that free advice is worth exactly what we've paid for it. Folks have opinions and some feel better about themselves by bashing others, so while you might see a negative review from time-to-time most of them are not worth the electrons they're displayed on. It may go without saying, but many negative reviews aren't assessments of your work, they're opinion pieces. Here's an example from Amazon:

> "Why do I say 'Not my cup of tea?' Though very well written, and chucked full of nuggets, the book format bugs me. Each page has bit of Sun Tzu's *Art of War* at the top; below that may be a historical discussion, and the next page may have an opinion

about something. While I respect both these gentlemen, and their opinions, I'm so full of my own opinions that I struggle to read someone else's."

While we appreciate that reviewer's purchase, there's nothing actionable in what he wrote. It's about him, not us, and does nothing to make our work better. If you're going to read a review of your book, positive or negative, listen to what is being said and then measure it with this test: Does that comment make you better? Is there a takeaway from which you can learn?

Stanley Kubrick, director of *2001, A Space Odyssey*, *The Shining*, and many other phenomenal works had an error in his Academy Award-winning film *Spartacus*. If you look closely, a rebellious slave in his movie is wearing a wristwatch. Does that small glitch take away from the fact that *Spartacus* was the 1961 Oscar nominee for best film editing? No.

A Negative Platform Tendency

Human beings are built on a negative platform. Most of us learn at a young age that touching a hot stove is painful. As a result of that negative feedback, we avoid the pain by not touching hot stoves. It's a survival instinct. Nevertheless, because of this negative platform tendency most folks go immediately to negative reviews and read them first. "Tell me why I don't want to touch this book, this metaphorical hot stove." They look for reasons not to buy. You're likely smiling as you know that you do the same thing too.

The good news is that most folks can see through jeweler loop reviews, realizing that the feedback is more about the reviewer than the book. So, if you're going to read reviews, scrutinize them for honest feedback and mentally flush the self-aggrandizing garbage.

Trusted and Untruthful Feeback

> "Wall Street is the only place that people ride to in a Rolls Royce to get advice from those who take the subway."
>
> — **Warren Buffett**

Solicit feedback, but not from your friends or family.

No Feedback is Better than Bad Feedback

"I need feedback, so I'll have my students look at this manuscript… and maybe a couple of friends."

If you go through a traditional publisher, they'll have you covered, but if you go the niche or self-publishing route then you are likely to desire feedback on your manuscript from your friends or family. That's a bad idea. First off, they like you and may not be fully candid in their response because they think it'll hurt your feelings. Second, they're not professional writers, editors, or reviewers. So, if you do ask folks to take an early read of your work, assure that whoever does the job has the requisite knowledge and experience to help you make it better. No feedback is better than bad feedback.

Seriously, your friends are going to lie to you. They're going to say that they like your manuscript simply because they like you. Friends, relatives, and students are horrible sources for constructive feedback. Your friends don't want to make things awkward; they want to have you invite them over for that summer BBQ. Your students are going to lie to you.

Subordinates Will Lie

As a rule, anybody who is subordinate to you in rank, organization, or club hierarchy who is asked to review your work won't be fully truthful. They will kowtow to your higher position, your authority. They will suck up to you. At best they will be deferential, have little to say, and tell you that they like the book.

We have a friend who has published multiple books of his own accord. He writes technical manuals and gets paid a princely sum for his insight. He can communicate the complex code that he writes in everyday language and teach others to do the same work at a high level. He is also a martial artist who prides himself on clarity, directness, and the ability to have keen insight.

When given a copy of one of our manuscript drafts that had a glaring error in it, a cumbersome, unclear, and redundant section, our friend didn't comment on that portion of the work. After he returned the marked-up manuscript, Kris reread the work and discovered the part that needed editing even though our friend had skated over that section.

When ask, the friend replied, "Yeah, I was wondering if you guys were going to fix that, but I didn't want to say anything."

Ouch! That's not what we asked for. We asked for harsh judgment and honest constructive feedback, but as a friend, he couldn't bring himself to do that even though he knew it wouldn't hurt our feelings, only help us get better.

Take this as a warning. It's what will happen if you give your book to a friend, relative, or student for review. Even your most trusted allies will not want to hurt you, and in doing so they inadvertently make things worse.

Professionals Provide Perception

Lawrence has friends who are luminary science fiction, fantasy, and speculative fiction authors, names you'd recognize if you're a fan of that genre. To get past the challenge of milquetoast, dissembling feedback, they form writers' groups, working together with authors and editors in their area to continuously improve each other's work.

Colleagues can take a more professional approach to beta reviews than friends, relatives, or subordinates can. Not only do they share tips and tricks of writing, but they also aggregate feedback from multiple perspectives when reviewing each other's manuscripts. In that fashion they're able to keep things timely, relevant, and constructive.

In fiction writing, authors have a tendency do glorious worldbuilding and character development early on only to rush to conclusion at the end of a book or series, much like what the producers of *Game of Thrones* did which for many fans ruined that streaming series. That's one of many things that the writers' group looks for in providing discerning feedback. It goes far beyond grammar and punctuation which are table stakes, focusing on plot continuity, characterization, story arc, readability, etc.

Your exact approach will vary depending on if you're writing fiction or non-fiction, and whether you're working with a traditional publisher, a niche publisher, or going the self-publishing route. Nevertheless, the goal is to solicit discerning feedback from professionals who have the knowledge, skill, and ability to help you put the best possible work out into the marketplace.

Cover Art

"Aspiring authors, get this through your head. Cover art serves one purpose, and one purpose only, to get potential customers interested long enough to pick up the book to read the back cover blurb. In the internet age that means the thumbnail image needs to be interesting enough to click on. That's what covers are for."

— Larry Correia

"Ooh, that speaks to me."

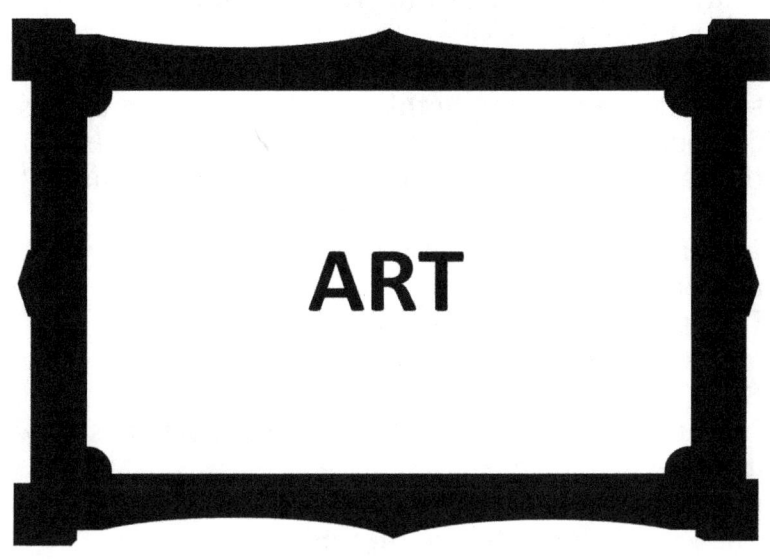

A Steaming Pile of Garbage

A martial artist from a *dojo* a couple of towns away had written a book. It was his first foray into publishing, and he was excited about the project. The book was personal, it contained many emotional stories as well as tactical and technical advice. This new author asked if Kris would look at his book for him.

Kris responded, "I will, and I will be honest with you. If it's good, I'll tell you. If it's bad, I'll tell you that too. Are you okay with that?"

"I wouldn't have it any other way."

A few nights later the new author passed his book across the *dojo* reception area and into Kris's hands. They both sat down, and Kris began to review the book cover.

"Who came up with this cover?"

"The publisher did."

"Did you go through a self-publishing service?"
"Yes."
"Okay. This is the cover they recommended to you?"
"Yeah, I like it."

It was a picture of a waterfall in a rainforest. Kris pointed out that the image had nothing to do with martial arts. His friend began to rationalize the decision made for him by the outfit he'd worked with, saying "Well, it's an expansive book. It's difficult to put a hard picture on it."

"I get that, but what does a waterfall have to do with what you wrote?"

"Oh, you know it's kind of *Zen* stuff."

"Would you humor me with a little test?"

"Sure."

Kris held the book up, "If this were a movie poster would you go see this movie?"

After a pause, "No, no I wouldn't."

"Then you should change the cover."

He didn't change the cover. And, that book languishes with no sales. Is that the only reason that the book isn't selling? Probably not, but the cover is the metaphorical front porch for the book, the place where he's inviting readers in. If they're turned away by a steaming pile of garbage at the threshold it doesn't really matter what's inside.

We've had some covers that failed too. At the time we produced them we thought they were bang-on, but in retrospect they were not. And, we've gone back and changed them. Yes, we listen to our own advice.

Stand Out from The Crowd

As of this writing there are 6,400 kindle books in the martial arts category on Amazon alone, so standing out from the crowd can be a real challenge. Think about simple stuff like colors. Every martial artist seems to want to use red, white, and black on their book cover, and we have as well. Here's an example:

You can google the psychology of colors to learn how they evoke emotions, exploring the idea in greater detail than we will present here, but in summary the answer is probably what you've already guessed at the gut-instinct level. Red equals passion, white denotes virtue, and black indicates power. Passion, virtue, and power, when thinking about martial arts that sounds about right doesn't it? The challenge is that everybody does that.

Think hard about your choice, oftentimes it means your book will get lost in the shuffle. Ours did.

Jump onto Amazon or some other online bookseller and look at top sellers in each category, not just martial arts but also category-adjacent genre like sports, philosophy, or self-help. Compare and contrast movie posters and streaming show ads for inspiration too.

No matter what you choose, your cover art must resonate with the potential reader, showing how it will answer their burning question, solve their urgent need, or fulfill their unmet desire. And it must stand out from the crowd. After all, its goal is to spark enough interest to inspire the prospective reader to learn more.

Who Was it Written For?

Let's do a brief thought experiment... Here are a couple of covers to compare. One was created by our in-house designer whereas the other was produced by an Italian publishing house for a translation of one of our books. What audience do you think each book was written for? What makes it resonate for that readership? How does it stand apart from other titles that cover the same subject matter? Does the cover spark your interest in learning more? Why or why not? How can you apply that insight to your own work?

Another martial artist came to us for advice. We pointed out that the cover for his self-defense book looked like the movie poster from the classic, *The Day the Earth Stood Still*. The cover screamed science fiction, not self-defense. His response, "Yeah, other people said that too." He paused, then continued, "But I worked hard on that cover. I'm not going to change it."

Nobody gives a rip about how hard he worked. They don't care how hard you work. And they don't care about how hard we worked either. All they care about is whether the work product sparks their interest. If not, you've failed.

Get your cover right.

Audio Books

"There's a world of a difference between reading and hearing. I mean, you extract the same juice out of the fruit of knowledge—whether it's coming off pod or page. But with audio, I like hearing the sound of someone else's voice. I like having a guide with me through the maze."

— **T.L. Huchu**

"I'm busy I don't have time to read. Unless, of course, you'd read it to me…"

The Author's Voice

While a few titles are available in hardcover, most of our books are only sold in softcover, e-book, and audiobook. Audiobooks are the smallest portion of our sales, currently just 5.9%, but they are the fastest growing channel too, and we expect them to account for an ever-increasing percentage of our sales over time.

Consequently, all our new releases have audio versions, and we went back and produced audio copies of our back catalog too. Some of those books were narrated by professional voice artists, while others we did ourselves, with Kris doing the voiceovers.

"I bought your book. I was disappointed that you didn't narrate it yourself."

We have had conversations with multiple people who purchased those books and every single one of them said something along the lines of, "I want to hear the author's voice, listen to their inflection. I want to hear their interpretation of what's going on in the book."

A noteworthy dynamic is that readers often start with an audiobook, and when they like it, they decide to purchase the paperback version too. For "fluff" reading like novels things are different, readers mostly pursue e-books and audiobooks. In the martial arts genre, on the other hand, readers often want the paperback or hardcover version for two reasons, to own the physical book as well as to mark it up for future reference so that they can have it readily available on their bookshelf.

There's a tactile element to a printed book that is difficult to get away from. Consequently, if you're going to publish a martial arts-related paperback or e-book, you'd best be able to convert it to audio too. You'll reach a much larger audience that way.

Since folks want to hear from the author, not an anonymous AI-generated speech processor or voice actor, it's best to do the narrating yourself. A corollary benefit is that reading the book aloud can improve your quality assurance process, finding any residual typos or unclarities you may have missed on the screen, so creating the audio version before finalizing the print and/or e-book is valuable.

Our workflow includes "finalizing" the manuscript, creating the audiobook, identifying any errors or unclarities discovered during that process, and then updating the manuscript once again before publishing. You would do well to emulate that process, but doing so requires access to a recording studio. There are a couple of ways to accomplish that, you can rent or build your own.

Studio Time Isn't Cheap

Professional studios are exceptional but expensive. Most of them charge an hourly rate that ranges from roughly $50 per hour up to well over $360, depending on where you live. In the Puget Sound region near Lawrence, for example, budget-priced studios that are conducive to audiobook creation run from $75 to $130 per hour. Higher-end locations whose services include editing, not just recording, often charge over $1,000 an hour.

The average audiobook contains about 10 hours of content, but you cannot power through and record all that in one sitting. It's challenging work, your energy will fade, and you'll do numerous retakes as you stumble through things. Consequently, the idea that you can record your book in a day or two is simply not realistic, even though you wrote it and intimately know the contents.

To get 10 hours of solid output, especially the first time you try, tends to take two- to three-times that long in studio, sometimes more. Even at cut-rate pricing, that's a couple of thousand dollars out of pocket, and you still have to do post-processing and editing afterward.

So, what did we do? Well, after thoughtful consideration we decided it was best to build our own studio.

How to Build Your Own Studio

We use an acoustically deadened room that's dedicated to audiobook and podcast recording, with walls covered by acoustic foam tiles. If you decide to go that route too, we recommend Fstop Labs Acoustic Panels in 2" x 12" x 12" foam. They're easy to apply and the two-inch depth is necessary for proper sound-dampening. Don't skimp and purchase something thinner. It won't work correctly.

Our current microphone is an Audio-Technica AT2020 Cardioid Condenser Studio XLR Microphone. You can spend less, but it will show in the final product. There are comparable microphones available from numerous other brands, but as of this writing, we believe that the AT2020 is the best value model from a price versus performance perspective.

Our mic stand is an InnoGear Mic Stand Desk, Adjustable Desktop Microphone Stand Table with Shock Mount Mic Clip Pop Filter 3/8" to 5/8" Adapter for Blue Yeti. Whichever stand you choose to buy, be sure to include a pop filter with your setup.

Without one you'll introduce all kinds of unwanted noise simply by speaking and breathing, and that will degrade the quality of your recording, which risks keeping your book from meeting the parameters necessary to get published. If you cannot meet parameters, you have wasted your time. No one will ever hear your book.

Our audio interface is a Focusrite Scarlett 2i2 3rd Gen USB Audio Interface. It's simple and easy to use. We started using Focusrite around 2015 and have found every generation of products they produce to be solid and dependable. This quality is shown in the reviews of our work.

For your recording program, we recommend FL Studios. It has a steep learning curve, but the ability to manage the quality of your recording using that software is hard to beat. Audacity, a freeware recording program, will suffice, but it has severe limitations by comparison. Nevertheless, the price is right and the learning curve shallow if you're not technically inclined or willing to invest time in learning FL Studios.

That's what we did, but we produced a ton of books and expect to continue to do so. We also do numerous interviews, podcasts, and the like, so that studio gets used enough to warrant the expense. That might not be your best route, especially if you expect to be a "one-and-done" author. In that case, we recommend having someone record the book for you.

Hiring a Professional Narrator

If you find the right narrator, it can make your life easier. There are multiple flaming hoops that you must jump through to get an audio file recorded properly, and folks who do it for a living know how to make it happen right. You'll receive the files in a manner that assures that all the audio thresholds of your publisher are met. Be forewarned, those requirements are strict and failing to meet even a single parameter will make it impossible to distribute your audiobook until you get it up to specification.

ACX (Audio Creation Exchange) is the audiobook side of Amazon publishing. Like other publishers, their audio submission requirements help assure top quality publications, and once you submit your book through their process a rigorous review is launched to assure that all their parameters are met. Examples include:

- ⇨ Audiobooks must have consistent overall sound and formatting (e.g., all mono or all stereo files)
- ⇨ All files must be free of extraneous sounds such as plosives, mic pops, mouse clicks, audible breathing, and outtakes (which is what the pop filter is for)
- ⇨ Audiobooks must include opening and closing credits that match the title's cover art and metadata
- ⇨ Each audio file must contain only one chapter or section
- ⇨ Each file must have no more than five seconds of room tone at its beginning and end
- ⇨ Each file must contain a section header
- ⇨ Each file must measure between -23dB and -18dB RMS[12]
- ⇨ Each file must have peak values no higher than -3dB
- ⇨ Each file must have a noise floor no higher than -60dB RMS
- ⇨ Each file must be 192kbps or higher 44.1kHz MP3, CBR[13]
- ⇨ Each file must be no longer than 120 minutes in length

These parameters can and do change from time-to-time, so you need to double-check them with each project. For example, another rule listed on ACX at the time of this writing is, "Unless otherwise authorized, your submitted audiobook must be narrated by a human." Since Amazon just launched a beta to create audiobooks using a virtual voice on their Kindle Direct Publishing site, one would presume that the service is authorized, but other sources of AI voice generation are not.

---

12   RMS, or root mean square, refers to the electrical power your audio signal creates over time.

13   CBR means constant bit rate. CBR, as opposed to variable bit rate (VBR), makes files easy for customers to play and quick to load since everything is constant from start to finish.

As you can see, the process is complicated. And professional narrators can help. So, how do you find someone? To begin you can look on ACX, an all-in-one marketplace for independent creators, where you can both hire a narrator and publish your audiobook. An alternative is Fiverr or similar freelance services marketplace like Upwork, Voquent, PeoplePerHour, or Voices, but you'll need to make sure that the voice actor you choose has a quality recording studio and can product ACX compatible files (or whatever audiobook publisher you choose to use) that meet all parameters. Another resource is the Professional Audiobook Narrators Association.

Look for someone that has the accent, articulation, pitch, projection, volume, inflection, and speech rate fit your materials. For example, the narrator we hired for *Sh!t Sun Tzu Said* sounds a lot like Michael Dorn, the actor who played Worf on *Star Trek*. Although the voice work was spot on and what we required, in retrospect, we should have narrated that ourselves, listeners prefer the author over any voice actor, but he did a great job.

For better or worse, the sound of the narrator's voice makes a powerful impression on listeners, so if you do decide to hire someone get samples of their work, conduct an interview, and choose carefully. You'll be working hand-in-glove throughout the process, and you'll need someone who's not only articulate but also prompt and professional. Many artists are challenged to meet deadlines.

No matter who you use to narrate your book, if you use foreign terms, such as Japanese terminology ubiquitous to martial arts, you'll need to create phonetic cheat sheets for your storyteller and work interactively to ensure that they pronounce everything correctly. That's one of the downsides to our genre, folks who don't practice martial arts often don't understand it.

If you think that you're going to have AI do your audiobook, you're not. Although the technology is increasingly getting better, it's still not ready for prime time. Listeners will know, and they will reject your work.

You Need a Website — Not!

> "Web design is not just about creating pretty layouts. It's about understanding the marketing challenge behind your business."
>
> — **Mohamed Saad**

New authors rarely derive value from their website.

.COM

Websites can be a great way for authors to market and sell their books, but only in limited circumstances. Typically, that involves social media marketing, click funnels (or call funnels for big ticket items), and a wide range of products or services that drive revenue beyond their book. Since you are likely supporting a single book, or possibly one you're written and a couple more in the hopper, this approach is not for you.

Our Website Didn't Work

We've been down that road. We were committed. Our website had all the bells and whistles, and in all directions. We will spare you the list, but know that it was expensive, multimedia, and professionally done. And, after four years, we couldn't point to a single book we sold because of our website. Sure, fans spent time there, but they bought through Amazon.com.

Amazon is the master of that domain. Like ours, your website will make no impact. The important elements of a website for book sales have been distilled, refined, and perfected by Amazon, then sweetened and packaged. Amazon does everything you need better than you can do it yourself.

Amazon does one-click sales. It ensures delivery. It supports both marketing and advertising, recommending your book to others using a proprietary algorithm mathematically designed to maximize sales. All this has nothing to do with you, they do it so they make more money for themselves, but you profit from it anyway. We needn't go on; suffice it to say that they have every metric covered.

The Marquee Exception

Marquee authors are unique, an exception to this rule. Marquee authors have a name that most folks recognize. The idea of a "marquee" comes from the film industry. If the star of a movie's name goes above the title of the movie, the star is the box office draw, not the film.

Only the rarest of the rare in the movie industry are marquee names, folks like Brad Pitt, Morgan Freeman, Robert Downey Jr, Samuel L. Jackson, and Tom Cruise. The same principle applies to authors and their books as well, folks like Danielle Steel, Dean Koontz, John Grisham, J. K. Rawling, and Stephen King. You are not a marquee name, nor despite all our successes, are we.

Our friend Barry Eisler, a New York Times bestselling author, has a website. His site contains his books, bio, and numerous other links. Those links create an immersive experience for his readers. Notice that we said "readers;" his site is designed for people who already are aware of his work, and they are legion. He's the guy who famously turned down a $500,000.00 contract with St. Martin's Press to self-publish his book *The Detachment*, becoming the "face" of self-publishing in the early days of CreateSpace (now KDP).

Eisler's book *Rain Fall* was made into a feature film starring Gary Oldman and Akira Emoto by Sony Pictures Japan. His website has his event schedule, upcoming projects, and even a section that outlines the mistakes he has made in his creative work.

You're not marquee. You're not Barry. And neither are we. Follow our example and let Amazon do the work for you. It will save you enormous time, money, and heartache.

How You Publish Matters

"Some books and authors are best sellers, but most aren't. It may be easier to self-publish than it is to traditionally publish, but in all honesty, it's harder to be a best seller self-publishing than it is with a house."

— **Amanda Hocking**

"I like to communicate using semaphore. If you don't understand the flags, that's your problem."

Barry Eisler is the "classic" example of a hybrid author. He started out working with a traditional publisher before going independent. We're hybrid authors, we've published through traditional, non-traditional, and independent press, and we each have one solo book that's self-published too. In this chapter we'll compare the options and help you decide which approach is right for you...

The Big Boys of Publishing

Traditional publishers include both the Big Five as well as a variety of smaller companies whose business models are to invest in promising authors and do the heavy lifting of getting their work out into the world. The author creates the IP, while the publisher does the design, layout, copyediting, proofreading, marketing, advertising, printing, digital delivery, copyright registration, distribution, publicity, etc.

The Big Five include Hachette Book Group, HarperCollins, Macmillan Publishers, Penguin Random House, and Simon & Schuster. Examples of smaller "traditional" publishers include Autumn House Press, Bellevue Literary Press, Big Luck Books, Black Lawrence Press, C&R Press, Press 53, Red Hen Press, Tiny Fox Press, Tupelo Press, and Unnamed Press, among others.

Here's a topline comparison between going through a traditional publisher[14] versus self-publishing[15] your work: The more famous you are, the better your odds of success with traditional publishing whereas the more passionate you are, the better your odds of success through self-publishing.

For traditional publishing, celebrity matters. It's hard to get a contract with a traditional publisher if you reach out to them. You can't even contact them directly. You will need to complete your manuscript and submit a polished proposal to a literary agent, who in turn pitches your book idea to the publisher's acquisition department.

If they're interested, you will need to successfully negotiate a contract (often aided by your agent and/or attorney), then work with the publisher and their team throughout the entire process. Conversely, it's much easier to get a book deal if the publisher reaches out to you. That more-or-less jumps you straight to the contract negotiation phase of the process.

Vegas Isn't the Only Place to Gamble

Typically, the deal you negotiate with a traditional publisher will include an advance, an upfront payment detailed in your contract as an amount that's held against future royalties. This means the publisher is betting that the project will be profitable for everyone involved, earning way, way more

---

14   For brevity we'll use the term "traditional publisher" as an umbrella for all the variations, including Big Five, niche, and independent press.

15   Self-publishing includes aggregators like KDP, BookBaby, Draft2Digital, Smashwords, Google Play Books, and IngrahamSpark as well as distribution channels like Amazon, Audible, Books-A-Millian, Rakuten Kobo, and Scribd.

than they shell out upfront accounting for both the advance and all production costs.

So, they're investing both in you personally as well as paying for the entire process of taking your manuscript, turning it into a finished book, publicizing it, and distributing it to the public. That's an expensive proposition, one that relies heavily on your brand/reputation for success. Advances alone can be high, and for marquee names they are considerable. For example:

- ⇨ In 2004, former president Clinton received a $15M[16] deal from Knopf for his autobiography *My Life*
- ⇨ In 2009, James Patterson signed a $150M deal with Hachette to write 17 books, the biggest book deal in history
- ⇨ In 2014, Hilary Clinton received $14M from Simon & Schuster for her book *Hard Choices*
- ⇨ In 2016, Bruce Springsteen received a $10M advance from Simon & Schuster for his autobiography *Born to Run*

Jackpot, Bullseye, Windfall... or Just Plain Luck

For self-publishing, passion, drive, and a little luck matter the most. For example, in 1931, Irma Rombauer spent half her life savings printing copies of *The Joy of Cooking*. Five years later Bobbs-Merrill Company acquired the rights to her book, and it has sold over 18 million copies worldwide today. E. L. James' bestseller *Fifty Shades of Grey* began as *Twilight* fan fiction. After self-publishing her book in 2012, she sold the film rights and it went on to become a hit movie in 2015, grossing over $166M.

As of 2023, the top ten bestselling self-published books include:

1. *Rich Dad Poor Dad* by Robert Kiyosaki
2. *The Tale of Peter Rabbit* by Beatrix Potter
3. *Building a Winning Career* by William Cowan
4. *Still Alice* by Lisa Genova

---

16   That advance would be roughly $22M in today's dollars.

5. *The Joy of Cooking* by Irma Rombauer
6. *The Martian* by Andy Weir
7. *Choose Yourself!* by James Altucher
8. *Eragon* by Christopher Paolini
9. *A Naked Singularity* by Sergio De La Pava
10. *Someone Has to Be the Most Expensive, Why Not Make It You?* by Andrew Griffiths

These ten books were all successful because of high-quality content, professional editing and design, and effective marketing. Let's face it, all bestselling books need those three things, and you probably don't know how to do them yourself. Consequently, the way you publish makes accomplishing those tasks harder or easier for you. And your choice either shifts the risk to someone else or places it firmly in your own lap.

Here are some key differences between the two approaches:

Traditional Publishing	Self-Publishing
⇨ The publisher owns the royalties and pays you ⇨ The publisher usually pays you an advance against royalties ⇨ The publisher has creative control ⇨ The publisher invests to assure professionalism, fact-checking, and copyright protection ⇨ Your book gets a prestigious ISBN ⇨ The publisher has the ability to circumvent some channel rules ⇨ Most publishers mandate that you hire an agent and you work through them ⇨ The process from manuscript to publication takes significantly longer, typically a minimum of 2 to 3 years ⇨ The publisher can facilitate marketing, advertising, and publicity (but you still have to actively participate)	⇨ You own the royalties (sans channel residual) and pay yourself ⇨ You earn nothing until you generate royalties ⇨ You have creative control ⇨ You must invest to assure professionalism, fact-checking, and copyright protection ⇨ Your book gets a less prestigious ISBN ⇨ You must religiously follow all distribution channel rules ⇨ You generally do not need an agent or attorney (with some exceptions) ⇨ The process from manuscript to publication is much shorter, typically between 1 week to 6 months ⇨ You do all the marketing, advertising, and publicity yourself, or hire someone

Our Story

What did we do? Well, we started with traditional publishing. Our first several books were produced by a niche company that focused primarily on martial arts-related works, and we enjoyed working with them. They were professional, had a highly respected ISBN in the genre, and handheld us throughout the process, which was a terrific learning experience. The challenge is that while our contract stated we'd be earning 15% royalties from our work, an amount that varied a bit depending on the distribution channel, we discovered that we only took home a mere 2.2%.

That publisher wasn't run by crooks, but the book industry has arcane rules, much like "Hollywood accounting," which works in their favor. For instance, the publisher's distributor took the same cut regardless of whether a work was produced in hardcover, softcover, or e-book, which makes no sense based on the underpinning costs of each distribution channel, yet that's what they had negotiated and we couldn't do anything to change it.

After deciphering the math, we decided to cut ties and go another route. That turned out to be harder than expected.

You see, our contract was "boilerplate," the same deal they offered to all their talent, and among other things, it came with an auto-renewing "right of first refusal" clause. That clause meant that the publisher had the option to accept or reject any book-length work we came up with, and we were not allowed to go to another publisher or do things ourselves without prior permission or we'd be in breach of contract. As bestselling authors, they weren't keen to let us go, so that could have led to a lawsuit if we hadn't handled things just right.

Lawrence, who negotiates contracts for a living, found us an out. The clause specified the next book-length work. It did not say anything about genre. So, he wrote an urban fantasy novel, one that he knew that a martial arts publisher would be completely uninterested in and used their rejection to get out of that auto-renewing agreement.

Despite positive reviews, including from the Paranormal Romance Guild, *Blinded by the Night* wasn't a bestseller, but that wasn't the point. The reason he wrote it was to create a contractually compliant way of escaping an unacceptably low royalty structure. The bloody stake on the cover relates to both supernatural characters in the story as well as to metaphorically putting a stake through the heart of a bad book deal.

After one of our martial arts books became an Amazon bestseller, it attracted attention from one of the Big Five publishing houses who reached out and asked us to do a book for them. That was cool, or so we thought until we went through the process of negotiating a contract. They were used to authors literally begging to be brought into the fold and didn't know what to do when we pushed back on their unreasonable requirements.

Contracts From the Age of Magellan

For example, their boilerplate contract required two typewritten copies of the manuscript and a digital copy in a format deemed suitable by the publisher. Under the terms of the proposed agreement, we'd only know whether the files we sent in were acceptable after sending a certified letter to their legal department and obtaining a written response in return.

That contract template appeared to have been written before the internet was invented and made no sense in the age of technology. First off, we didn't own a typewriter, hence couldn't produce typewritten copies, so we asked them to change that language to specify printed documents instead. They refused.

We asked them to stipulate what digital medium they wanted, Word, Adobe PDF, or whatever, and what version of the software was required. Again, they refused. They'd offered up an advance that could have purchased a starter home in the Midwest and couldn't understand why we weren't willing to immediately sign on the dotted line, while we, on the other hand, were disinclined to endorse an agreement that would have placed us in breach of contract before we even started working with them.

Long story short, after 14 months of painful negotiations we finally reached an agreement. Lawrence has negotiated multibillion-dollar IT outsourcing deals in less time and more amicably.

The book was released a few years later and did reasonably well in the marketplace, in part due to the marketing and promotion the publisher did on our behalf, but because we were required to go through a literary agent who literally did nothing of value on our behalf but took a substantial cut anyway, the royalties weren't worth the pain. All-in-all we wouldn't work with them again.

So, the niche publisher didn't pay well enough, and the big publishing house was a royal pain in the butt to work with. We needed to find an alternative and ultimately ended up founding our own company, Stickman Publications, Inc. It's a C-corporation, which carries a more prestigious ISBN than self-publishing, yet still gives us full creative control. The risk and reward are both ours, yet by leveraging what we learned along the way and bringing along our pre-existing fanbase we've done all right.

Your Story

So, you've heard our story. What's yours? Think about the best path to publish your book. While you're doing that, know that there are a lot of scams in the publishing industry. Do your homework carefully before engaging with anyone, no matter whether it's a traditional publisher, independent publisher, aggregator, or self-publishing outlet.

Here are some examples, nothing close to the full list, of your choices:

Traditional Publishers	Independent Publishers	Self-Publishing Aggregators	Self-Publishing Retail Channels
• Major Publishers: • Hachette Book Group • HarperCollins • Macmillan Publishers • Penguin Random House • Simon & Schuster • Niche Publishers: • Autumn House Press • Bellevue Literary Press • Big Luck Books • Black Lawrence Press • C&R Press • Press 53 • Red Hen Press • Tiny Fox Press • Tupelo Press • Unnamed Press	• Akashic Books • Alternating Current Press • Algonquin Books • BOA Editions • Catapult Books • City Lights Publishers • Coffee House press • Enchanted Lion Books • Europa Editions • Featherproof Books • George Braziller • Graywolf Press • Hawthorne Books • Kensington Publishing • Mango Publishing • McSweeney's Books • New Directions Publishing	• Amazon KDP • Apple Books • Barnes & Noble Press • BookBaby • Draft2Digital • Google Play Books • IngrahamSpark • Rakuten Kobo • PublishDrive • Smashwords • StreetLib • XinXii	• Amazon.com • Audible • Apple Books • Baker & Taylor • Barnes & Noble • Bibliotheca • Bookmate • Books-A-Million • Blio • Google Play • Hugendubel • Odilo • OverDrive • Indigo • Playster • Rakuten Kobo • Scribd • Smashwords • Tolino

If you choose to go your own route, you'll also need to engage with service providers for editing/proofreading, copyright protection, formatting, indexing, ISBN registration, legal services, manuscript evaluation, marketing, promotional materials, translation services, audiobook narration, website design (if necessary), and the like.

Examples of author service providers include Bookbub, Fiverr, Kindlepreneur, Reedsy, and Written Word Media. A great resource to find and vet folks who do that type of work is the Alliance of Independent Authors (https://selfpublishingadvice.org/).

Protect Your Copyright

"The public feels that if it's on the Internet and you can access it, you deserve it. You haven't committed any kind of crime. We may even have to rename piracy. But in any case, we have to confront it."

— **Morgan Freeman**

Thieves are prone to steal, but you don't need to leave your door unlocked to make it easy.

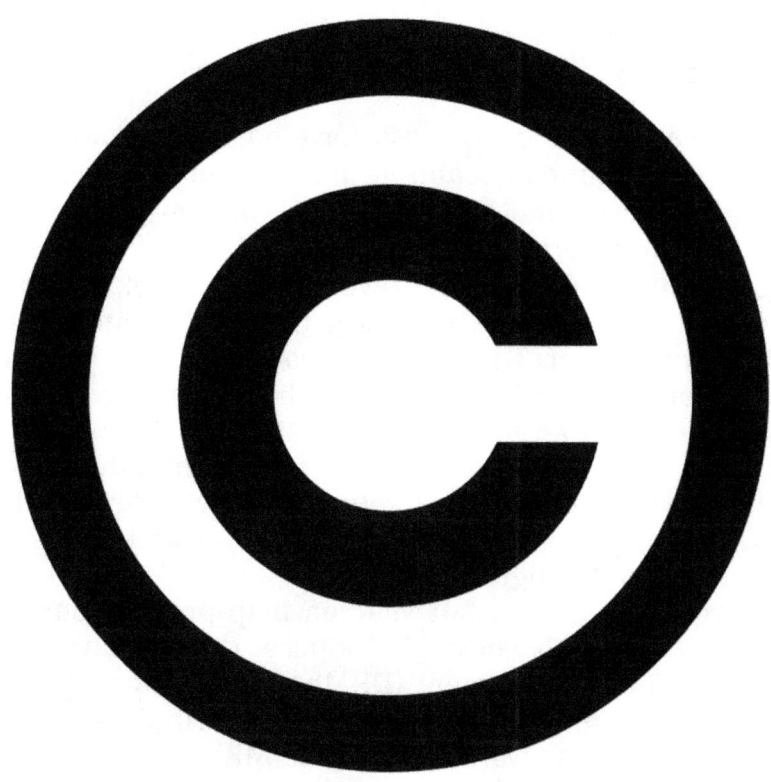

There were 16.5 million unlawful book downloads in the United States in 2017, and although validated statistics are hard to come by that number appears to be growing rapidly, with projections as high as 83.5% per year. Popular illegal download sites include 1337X, 4shared.com, upload.net, and bookos.org, among many, many others, with 17,380,000,000 visits in 2023 collectively.

While those dishonest sites carry the highest risk, it is important to monitor Google books, Amazon, and other legitimate sources for pirated copies of your work too. We've found numerous instances of "autographed" copies of our books appearing on Amazon, many selling for 4 to 5 times the cover price, and every one of them was fake. We've never sold signed copies there. The good news is that Amazon is quick to remediate the grey market and counterfeit products on its site.

Batten Down the Hatches, Matey

Piracy has always been a risk for e-books and audiobooks, but with ubiquitous scanning and conversion technology even hardcover and softcover works are in jeopardy too. In 2021 the International Publishers Association reported over a billion dollars in lost revenue due to book piracy, but financial loss is not the only issue this theft creates.

In many instances illegal download sites don't even have a real copy of your book, it's a phishing scam, or they have created an adulterated version designed to inject viruses or malware that facilitates identity theft and other crimes. Younger readers are more likely to steal, with 88% of e-book pirates in the 18- to 44-year-old age group, and they're also a major target of digital criminals.

There's no panacea, but you can help protect your work from pirates with copyright notices, digital watermarks, digital rights management (DRM), and similar techniques, as well as by leveraging trustworthy distribution channels for releasing your work. The Digital Millennium Copyright Act can provide some degree of protection too, but in most instances, there's little you can realistically expect to accomplish other than making it a little more painful for pirates to steal your work.

Anything you write that becomes a bestseller will be bootlegged. That's a 100% certainty.

A few days after *The Little Black Book of Violence* became an Amazon bestseller, illegal copies popped up on dozens of sites around the world, and that was back in 2010. Things move much faster now. Our publisher had registered the ISBN and copyright and took prompt legal action, but it barely made a dent in the number of pirated copies. Their attorneys contacted website owners and host/DNS[17]

---

17   DNS stands for Domain Name System, a hierarchical and distributed naming convention for computers, services, and other resources on the Internet and other Internet Protocol networks.

providers, but for every illicit channel they shut down half a dozen more popped up.

Let's Not Make It Easy

That's depressing, but don't give up. Do everything you reasonably can to protect your intellectual property. Here are a few tips:

- ⇨ Never post your manuscript anywhere that's public
- ⇨ Thoroughly vet prospective agents, editors, and author service providers
- ⇨ Carefully screen anyone who sees your manuscript before it's published, especially beta readers
- ⇨ Register your ISBN and copyright
- ⇨ Create Google alerts for both your name and your book title(s) to monitor what's going on
- ⇨ Contact (or have your attorney contact) site owners and host/DNS providers and ask them to remove unlicensed content
- ⇨ Distribute your books worldwide (simple lack of access is one root cause of piracy)
- ⇨ Watermark your e-books
- ⇨ Leverage DRM

The bottom line: Do your best, but don't expect to stop all illicit activity. No matter what you do, you won't even come close. Consider pirated copies you can't shut down free advertising and move on.

Insider Info

> "I wrote a book. It sucked. I wrote nine more books. They sucked, too. Meanwhile, I read every single thing I could find on publishing and writing, went to conferences, joined professional organizations, hooked up with fellow writers in critique groups, and didn't give up. Then I wrote one more book."
>
> **— Beth Revis**

Everyone is looking for the easy way, the one quick trick.

There are a handful of additional tips and tricks that we've discovered the hard way over the years. They didn't fit in the other chapters, or would have made them too long, so we've listed them here...

Avoid Shadow-Bans

We mentioned earlier that traditional publishers can, on occasion, circumvent channel rules while self-published authors must follow all channel rules religiously. And we told you that a critical success factor is to produce an exceptional title that garners attention. Unfortunately, certain titles are an example of how these two factors can coalesce to cause you pain. It's called shadow-banning, and it hurts because people can't buy books they cannot find.

Sh*t My Dad Says is #1 New York Times bestselling book written by author Justin Halpern. It became a television series, with a two-year-run on CBS. If you look for that book on Amazon or any other online retailer you can find it easily. However, if you search for a book about *Shitō-ryu*, a martial style that's a synthesis of the Okinawan *Shuri-te* and *Naha-te* schools of karate, you'll need to know the exact title or hunt through the author's page to find it as the algorithm thinks that's a naughty word. If you try to write an Amazon or B&N review of a book on *Shitō-ryu* that includes the title, it'll be banned as a violation of community guidelines. We got trapped by their system too.

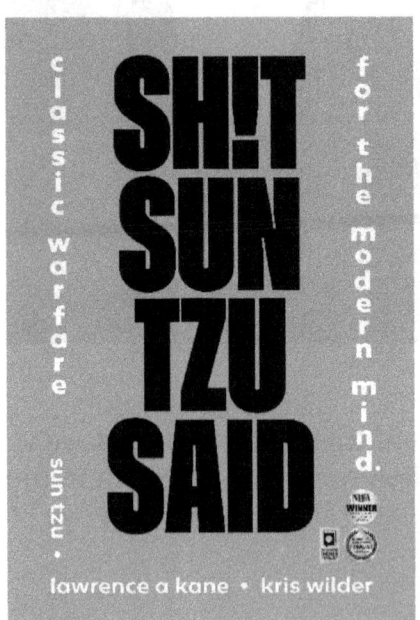

The book on the left and the book on the right are, for all intents and purposes, the same thing, modernizations of Sun Tzu's classic *Art of War*. While *Sh!t Sun Tzu Said* is a better title than *Clarity vs. Chaos*, and resonated far better with our fan base, it was nearly impossible for prospective readers to find it unless they searched for the exact phrase spelled correctly, including the exclamation point, because our book got shadow-banned.

Sh!t isn't a bad word, but it implies one, just like Sh*t does. When we contacted KDP they informed us that either spelling would result in our being sent to search engine purgatory, based on their channel rules. Nevertheless, Halpern got a pass because his publisher, HarperCollins, wasn't held to the same "rules."

So, if you go through one of the Big Five publishers, this won't be an issue. If you don't, however, be sure your book won't be trapped in search engine purgatory before you finalize your title.

Optimize Your Metadata

Every book you publish includes metadata that can help it sell. These keywords and phrases leverage the same algorithms that can shadow-ban certain titles, but in a good way. These tags, things like title, description, author(s), contributors, ISBN, publication date, audience/age-appropriateness, subject, qualifiers, genre, category, and subcategory, help prospective readers find your work. If you go through a traditional publisher, they'll do all that for you, but if you self-publish it can be tricky to identify the best keywords with which to list your book to bring it to the right people's attention.

Useful keywords can include descriptions of the setting, character types, roles, plot themes, or story tone. Anything designed to advertise, promote, or mislead readers, on the other hand, will likely get your title delisted. You only get a handful of user-controlled keywords to use, and they're difficult to retroactively change, so you need to get them just right. Tools like Publisher Rocket can be a great resource to help you do that.

External Website Links

Speaking of things changing, that's a risk if you use external website links in your e-books. You'll note that we've included a few in this book, but they're all associated with sites we're confident will be around for a long time. We didn't, for example, use links to the equipment we use for audiobook creation in the Audio Books chapter, which would have been convenient for you, but problematic for us.

You see, if a dead link pops up in an e-book, say because technology has evolved and the OEM de-lists earlier versions of their equipment, most publishers will take that book out of production until the link is fixed. It's a quality control process that helps assure happy customers. That's a good thing, but the challenge is that few publishers actually tell authors they've done that.

We found out about broken links the hard way when royalties suddenly disappeared, and we investigated why. On KDP it shows an error on your author dashboard, but not every publisher does even that. So, be careful when using external website links in your e-books. That won't harm softcover or hardcover formats, other than perhaps a nasty email or two from disgruntled readers who painstakingly type the links only to discover they don't work, but it's best that all versions of your work are always available. And annoying your readers rarely ends well.

Finally, if you do decide to include links, know that you're connecting to data that might change without your knowing it. For example, news stories and opinion pieces are often updated retroactively, which means what you read when you placed the link might be materially different than your readers will discover later on. Consequently, it's a best practice to include a disclaimer to help protect yourself and your reputation, something along the lines of, "Neither the author nor the publisher has any control over or assumes any responsibility for websites or external resources referenced in this book."

Safeguard Your Reputational Integrity

Your reputation is important, especially as a published author. Did you know that the Beauty Queen Killer's name was Chris Wilder? He abducted at least a dozen young women and girls, murdering eight of them during a six-week cross-country crime spree in 1984. Co-author Kris Wilder is a different person, but has an eerily similar name, one spelled with a "K" instead of a "C."

The Zodiac Killer was the pseudonym of a maniac who murdered five people in the San Francisco Bay area of Northern California in the late 1960s. Career criminal Lawrence Kane was a prime suspect for those unsolved homicides. Again, eerily like co-author Lawrence's identity, although the Zodiac Killer suspect was an older man who died on May 20, 2010.

So, we're Kris and Lawrence the authors, not the serial killers, and that's kind of an important distinction.

Reputation goes beyond being confused for someone else, it's a widespread belief about you that supersedes reality, hence the term "court of public opinion." Folks will buy your books if they are interested in the subject matter and imagine that they know you, like you, and trust you. Undermine that trust, ruin your reputation, and you'll kill your book sales. Your public persona should be intentioned and intentional, designed to reinforce your expertise in whatever field you're writing about.

You probably don't need a reputation manager like Hollywood celebrities do, but you should be cautious about staying on message when promoting your work and charitable efforts. Consistency matters. Scrub your social media, stay away from politics[18], and be careful about what you post online. You can proactively monitor what folks are saying about you too, if you so desire, but think twice and meticulously compose any messages before you respond. Unhinged social media rants, X/Twitter wars, and the like never make a good impression.

Book Signings are Resigned to the Dustbin of History

Several years ago, Lawrence flew to a conference in Orlando. Because it was a West coast to East coast cross-country flight, covering three time zones, he knew that he would have to run from the airport to the hotel with little time to spare

---

18   Unless that's your profession... Based on voting patterns, any political statement you make is likely to alienate as much as half the population, undermining KLT and cutting deeply into your sales base.

before giving his keynote presentation, so he wore a suit on the plane. After taking his seat he noticed the guy across the aisle noticing him, nodded in acknowledgment, and settled in for the flight. As they rolled out onto the runway that guy kept looking his way. It wasn't creepy, but it was odd, so Lawrence decided to ignore it.

After they reached altitude and the fasten seatbelt sign was turned off, the guy across the aisle opened the overhead bin, rummaged around in his backpack, and pulled out a book, *The Way of Kata*.

He looked at the back cover, stared hard at Lawrence once again and said, "You're wearing glasses and a suit, so I'm not totally certain, but are you, *Sensei* Kane?"

"Yes."

"I thought so! Would you be willing to autograph my book?"

We have done a variety of book signings at Barnes & Noble, Kinokuniya, University of Washington bookstore, and many others, but not for over a decade. That used to be a good way to meet and greet the public, sell a few books, and get your name out there, but book signings no longer attract clientele unless they're arranged by a traditional publisher (and rarely even then if you're not a marquee name).

If you want to take a few books with you to a seminar or conference, go right ahead, but know that most of the autographs you'll sign nowadays will be when folks bring your book to you, not the other way around.

The "Blue Screen of Death"

When we started writing this book Kris built the initial outline, fleshed out some of the contents, and then passed along his files and notes to Lawrence to continue working on. Lawrence, in turn, put about five hours into manuscript development, saved his work, and went out to run some errands. When he got back, he was shocked to discover Microsoft's dreaded blue screen of death. His laptop had crashed. While he was able to recover the device, the file he'd been working on became corrupted and was unusable. While that was frustrating, it was only one day's worth of work to recreate, but it brings up an important point about saving your work.

Everything you write should be backed up not only on your device but also in a secured cloud storage platform as well as on an external drive. Triple redundancy may seem like overkill but it's the best practice. A thumb drive is fine for most folks, but if you do a lot of books[19] we recommend a hot swappable diskless DAS, NAS, or RAID storage array such as those produced by Terramaster, Sabrent, or Satechi. That way you're protected not only against the dreaded blue screen of death, but also corrupted files, malware, ransomware, and other hazards that can destroy all your hard work.

Save your work often and use version control. The easiest way to do that is to add the date to the end of your filename throughout every iteration of the manuscript. For example,

---

19 Especially audiobooks which create very large files. Exact sizes vary depending on your format (e.g., MP3, MP4, WAV, DAISY, Enhanced EPUB), but you can expect sizes ranging from roughly 400MB up to several GB per book.

Punching-Up-03-14-24. Not only does this practice help you lose no more than one day's worth of work at worst should your file becomes corrupted, but it also plays well in court if you ever must deal with a plagiarism or copyright infringement lawsuit because you'll have comprehensive documentation around the evolution of your work product. We tend to call the final version either "final," "submission copy," or something similar to differentiate it from the working drafts. In this case, *Punching-Up-submission copy*.

Plagiarism

Speaking of plagiarism, that's a huge risk in our industry. Words and images are copyrighted, but even fonts can be too even though US law doesn't generally cover typefaces. Images, for example, can be public domain, free to use and share, free to use and share commercially, free to modify, share, and use, or free to modify, share, and use commercially.

An image licensed for commercial use allows the picture to be used for moneymaking activities on behalf of the person or company licensing it, so if you use an image for your cover or inside your book that you didn't take yourself and haven't purchased a commercial license for you open yourself up to a lawsuit. These licenses can be exclusive or non-exclusive, generally require image crediting, and are licensable with different types of legal agreements and payment structures.

Even if you snap the picture yourself, if there are any people in that image you've taken and wish to use in your book, you'll almost certainly need them to sign a model release to protect yourself. If you don't and your book does well, you can expect to have a process server show up at your door.

As you can see, it's complicated. Even if we don't fully understand all this stuff, we hire people who do. You should too.

Paying it Forward

"When you learn, teach.
When you get, give."

— **Maya Angelou**

You are responsible to and for the next generation.

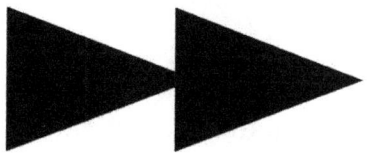

Due Diligence

Most accidents on Mt. Everest happen during the descent, not on the climb up the mountain. Mountaineers are tired, and they also can become content with their achievements. Call it a combination of lack of focus and physical exhaustion. This is a dangerous mixture, costing more than 300 people their lives.

Staying safe requires effort, and a methodical pace during the descent despite anticipation of being done with the journey. The same thing applies to you as an author nearing the end of your writing project.

Elected officials, athlete's, actors, and musicians all take pictures with people they don't know. Sometimes these photos are taken as part of a conference, fundraiser, or award ceremony, sometimes at extemporaneous moments. Celebrities are asked for autographs, to take selfies with strangers all the time, even when they're doing mundane things like going out to dinner.

There is difficulty in screening everybody, particularly with impromptu encounters such as at a restaurant. These popular people are unable to check the background of folks they take pictures with.

As the public, we understand this. If an actor takes a photo with a later-to-be-found criminal, we don't think too much of it. We dismiss it because we understand how the dynamics work. It's a picture, not an endorsement. They are not friends or even acquaintances, it's just a picture.

Some Folks Who Didn't Have to Care, but Did

We've been very fortunate. As aspiring writers, we signed with a niche martial arts publisher that was small enough to care about their talent and work hand-in-glove with us, yet simultaneously big enough to have market power and get our books out into the world. Among other things, they introduced us to other authors, and between those connections and our network of fellow martial artists we were able to build relationships with dozens of successful authors, folks like Alain Burrese, Barry Eisler, Bill Dietz, Dan Anderson, Gavin Mulholland, Iain Abernethy, Loren W. Christensen, Marc MacYoung, Martina Sprague, Peter Consterdine, Philip Starr, Rory Miller, Steve Perry, and many more.

They've contributed to our content, written blurbs showcasing our work, and told their friends about us. Some have beta-read our manuscripts and provided discerning feedback, and in some instances even gone so far as to have written forewords for our books.

With their help, we grew our reputation as writers faster and more effectively than we ever could have done alone. With their counsel, we eliminated a ton of trial and error in discovering everything we've shared with you in this book. In honor of those who helped us out, we're delighted to pay that goodwill forward, writing blurbs, forewords, book/article contributions, and other content for up-and-coming writers whom we think make the cut.

This is commendable, of course, and we recommend that you do the same once you're successful, but you need to be careful not to undermine your reputation with well-intentioned actions.

In other words, contributing to another author's work is not a random celebrity photo, it's your seal of approval, a direct association of you with their work. And that requires investigation. Do your research, ask questions, and be certain of who you're dealing with when it comes to blurbs, forewords, or other endorsements.

Damn, That Escalated Quickly

Lawrence was contacted by an author who asked if he would read his first book and endorse it if he liked what he had read. Lawrence agreed, and after reviewing the manuscript found that it was okay. The book wasn't outstanding, but it wasn't awful either, and the guy seemed like a nice person. He figured this new author could use some help and talked to Kris about it. Having adopted a "pay it forward" mindset, we both decided to help, writing blurbs for that author.

A second book by the same writer followed the next year. That book showed up at Lawrence's door unsolicited. The new book was autographed and personalized to him. There was also a handwritten request for an endorsement. We both looked and decided to pass because while the first book was acceptable for an initial offering that author had not gotten any better at his craft. Lawrence took responsibility to politely inform him that we wouldn't endorse his latest effort.

The budding author had assumed we had a relationship, which can happen, it's not the biggest issue. The second assumption, born out of that first assumption, was that we would rubber-stamp his new book. No. Our integrity is on the line for anything we endorse, and if it's not good we won't do it. Lawrence politely told him via email that we were going to pass on advocating that book but left an open offer to contact us in the future. Sadly, the author was not at all gracious when we turned him down.

He became infuriated. Acting as the manchild he was, he wrote a flaming email back to Lawrence. Among other things, the author requested that the personalized book he'd sent be returned. It was petulant anger, and surprising because we thought we knew him. Over time it became evident that this author was a fraud. He talked one game and behaved another. He was a paper tiger, one who had built a facade around himself.

We Assumed Goodwill... It Was a Mistake

Generosity had been afforded to us by other authors, and we thought we could, as we have said, pay it forward. We have with other people. Virtually every writer we have helped has been gracious, pleasant, and earnest in conducting themselves, regardless of whether we sanctioned their work because they realized that we were doing our best to make them better. But in that instance, we failed to do our due diligence and as a result wound up endorsing a mediocre book by a very nasty person.

It's the same with pretty much any endeavor. Kris worked with a consultant a few years back who tended to name-drop. That guy seemed to know everyone important in the industry and told stories about them, yet Kris knew a few of them too and some of that guy's claims seemed dubious. So, Kris picked up the phone and called one of his associates to see if that consultant was really who he said he was. It turns out that he didn't know the folks he claimed he did, not well enough to represent them at least. The call took five minutes and saved potential heartache. Kris cut ties with that guy. We wish we'd done the same with that manchild author.

Remain Vigilant

If you're asking for an endorsement, a foreword, or a contribution to your work, know who you're asking. If you're asked, know who is asking you. A few moments of cursory research on the internet will likely give you what you need. A phone call to a common associate is even better if you're able to do it. It takes only moments, but a little due diligence can save you a calendar of heartache.

It's not just endorsements from others. Mistakes can be made putting your book together, especially as it nears completion. The end is in sight, you're anxious to get it done, and you can get sloppy.

Never forget that most climbing accidents happen on the descent. Remain vigilant.

Conclusion

"Advice? I don't have advice. Stop aspiring and start writing. If you're writing, you're a writer. Write like you're a goddamn death row inmate and the governor is out of the country and there's no chance for a pardon. Write like you're clinging to the edge of a cliff, white knuckles, on your last breath, and you've got just one last thing to say."

— **Alan Wilson Watt**

We want to add one more quote from the fictional character, Ron Swanson from the television show Parks and Recreation:

"Never half-ass two things, whole-ass one thing."

There's far more to being a published author than having your name on a book cover, making a few bucks, or preserving knowledge. As writers we are fortunate to connect, to touch people's lives all around the world through our work. Often, we'll never know our impact with certainty, but from time-to-time readers contact us and share their stories.

If you publish something of note, create value for your readership, you'll experience the same thing too. We've received numerous letters and emails over the years. Here's a sample of some memorable ones:

> "I can't thank you enough. Someone gave me your book when they heard about what I was doing. I totally agree how women have a hard time 'seeing' themselves as doing these perceived 'nasty' moves. On a personal note, 10 years ago I was violently mugged, and let me tell you, now that I'm a mother, I've no problem integrating the idea of a seriously defensive type of action." — **Mishele**

> "I really like what you said about 'the more dangerous you are, the less you should feel the need to prove it.' I am going to make that mindset a part of me. Thank you!" — **Greg**

> "*Domo arigato*, I just read your book. I thought it was great information! I wish there were more books out there like this! I just started at the beginning to reread." — **Danny**

> "I'm a soccer hooligan. Was. My passion is starting fights, glassing people, but your *Little Black Book of Violence* made me reconsider. I am writing so you know your words made me think, inspired me to be better. I cut off my old mates and move to a new neighborhood. Thank you!" — **Geoff**

> "Hi there. I'm sure you get fan mail all the time, but I'm compelled to let you know how much I appreciate your books. I just finished *Uma* and think it's your best work yet. Sadly, it kept me from much needed sleep but was totally worth it." — **Patty**

> "Thank you for writing an excellent book. There are so many out there that profess to tell you that it can teach you to punch and kick properly and so few that deal mainly with the heart of *kata*. I have picked up the book and am currently pouring through it

as my busy schedule allows me. So far, I have found that it is well worth the money." — **Michael**

"I am a medical doctor and a practitioner of *Shotokan* karate since 1973, the time I earned my black belt. Honestly, I had been looking for reading materials about karate and stumbled into your book. It has helped me understand a lot of concepts why we do these *kata* exercises." — **Butch**

"Gentlemen, I found your book to be intelligent and sober. There are too few realistic books on the market today, many of which can lead a reader to make a mistake in dealing with the harsh reality of the street, etc. Thank you for your efforts in properly educating martial artists." — **John**

"Your admonishment to respond rather than react woke me up. I am that road rage guy. I cuss, I scream, I flip bad drivers off. In the safety of my truck, I never thought about what the other person might do until I read your book. From now on I will keep my anger to myself. Thank you, *Sensei*!" — **Adam**

"I enjoyed your book and am about to read it a second time. I have also been studying *kata* for a lengthy time and found that much of what you wrote parallels my own thinking, although we do have some differences. But as an old Chinese saying goes, 'If two men say exactly the same thing, only one man is thinking.'" — **Christopher**

"OMG, *The Way to Black Belt* is amazing! I earned my copy as *Sifu*'s student of the month last year and it was motivating as hell. I am rereading chapter 7 again while recovering from ACL reconstruction surgery now. Without your guidance on injuries, I probably would have quit after that accident. Incidentally, we do not use belts in *Choy Li Fut*, but I do aspire to wear a black-hued fringe on the end of my sash. You're the best!" — **Mei**

"Hi there. I would like to compliment you on your awesome book. I have been a student of karate for 37 years and like many others I have been baffled by *kata* and how it really works in relation to real combat. I can honestly say that after many years your book has answered my questions. Congratulations on this masterpiece!" — **Dan**

"You really made me think about fighting in a way that I never have before. I got a little queasy reading some of your examples and viewing some of your pictures was downright disturbing, thank God they are not in color, but I learned a LOT from the experience. And I know that I am better off for it." — **Joey**

"I know this is coming out of the blue, but I am writing to let you know that you saved my life! *Sifu* taught me how to fight, but never explained what comes after. If it wasn't for your book, I am certain that I would be in jail. Thank you so much! If you are ever in New York, look me up. I would be honored to buy you dinner." — **Sam**

Clearly, there are non-material benefits of being a published writer, not the least of which is establishing your legacy. The textbook definition of the word legacy is, "The lasting impact of particular activities, events, and actions that took place in the past," but that falls short in our view.

We prefer to think of it this way: If you approach each day with gratitude and enthusiasm, you will live a fulfilling life and leave a positive legacy. The challenge is that for most people only a handful of close associates know about it. Writing a book, better yet penning a catalog of books, this extends your reach a thousandfold. Folks you've never met, nor are likely to meet, can be impacted by what you've said and done.

Be safe. And be well.

Kris   Lawrence

About the Authors

Kris Wilder

Kris was inducted into the U.S. Martial Arts Hall of Fame in 2018. He runs the *Cheney Karate Academy*, a frequent destination for practitioners from around the world which also serves the local community. He has earned black belt rankings in three styles, *karate, judo,* and *taekwondo,* and often travels to conduct seminars across the United States, Canada, and Europe. His book, *The Way of Sanchin Kata*, was translated into Japanese, a rare honor for a Western *karate* practitioner.

A Nationally Board-Certified Life Coach and prolific author, Kris has lectured at Washington State University and Susquehanna University and served as an advisor for the Eastern Washington University *Karate* Club.

He spent about 15 years in the political and public affairs arena, working for campaigns from the local to national level. During this consulting career, he was periodically on staff for elected officials. His work also involved lobbying and corporate affairs. And, he was also a member of The Order of St. Francis (OSF), one of many active Apostolic Christian Orders.

Kris is the bestselling author of 32 books, including a Beverly Hills Book Award and Presidential Prize winner, a Living Now Book Award winner, a USA Best Book Awards winner, a National Indie Excellence Awards winner, three Independent Press Award winners, a Next Generation Indie Book Awards winner, and two Eric Hoffer award nominees. He has been interviewed on CNN, FOX, The Huffington Post, Thrillist, Nickelodeon, Howard Stern, and more.

Kris lives in Cheney, Washington. You can contact him directly or connect on social media here: https://linktr.ee/KrisWilder.

Lawrence A. Kane

Lawrence is Head of Procurement at a leading diversified financial services company in the United States. He was inducted into the SIG Sourcing Supernova Hall of Fame in 2018 for visionary leadership in strategic sourcing, procurement, supplier innovation, and digital transformation. In 2023 he earned an EPIC Award for lifetime achievements in indirect procurement from ProcureCon.

Over the course of his career, he institutionalized world-class practices that earned the prestigious Global Excellence in Outsourcing award from IAOP and three Future of Sourcing innovation awards from SIG, among other honors, and regularly advances thought leadership as a keynote speaker at industry conferences.

The bestselling author of 29 books, Lawrence has been a guest on nationally syndicated and local radio shows (e.g., The Jim Bohannon Show, Biz Talk Radio), television programs (e.g., Fox Morning News), and podcasts (e.g., Art of Procurement, Negotiations Ninja Podcast, Sourcing Industry Landscape), and has also been interviewed by reporters from *Information Week*, *Le Matin*, *CPO Strategy*, *Forbes*, *Jissen*, and *Computerworld*, among other publications.

Heavily involved in serving his community, he volunteers as a mentor with the Global Mentorship Initiative, MSIS program at the University of Washington, and other worthy organizations where he counsels college graduates entering the workforce, helps military personnel transition to the corporate world, and guides early career professionals through interviews and job progressions. In 2022, he was honored with a Top DEIB Leader Walk the Walk Award.

Lawrence has been studying and teaching martial arts since 1970, including a wide variety of traditional Asian styles, medieval swordsmanship, modern combatives, and close-quarters combat. He lives in Seattle, Washington. You can contact him at lakane@ix.netcom.com or connect on LinkedIn (www.linkedin.com/in/lawrenceakane).

Explore More from The Authors

Kris Wilder and Lawrence Kane are the bestselling, award-winning authors of *Musashi's Dokkodo, The Little Black Book of Violence, 10 Rules of Karate, Dude, The World's Gonna Punch You in the Face,* and *Martial Arts and Your Life,* among numerous other titles. Discover more below...

Kris Wilder

Lawrence A. Kane

www.ingramcontent.com/pod-product-compliance
Lightning Source LLC
Chambersburg PA
CBHW060319050426
42449CB00011B/2558